SpyBoy™
The M★A★N★G★A Affair

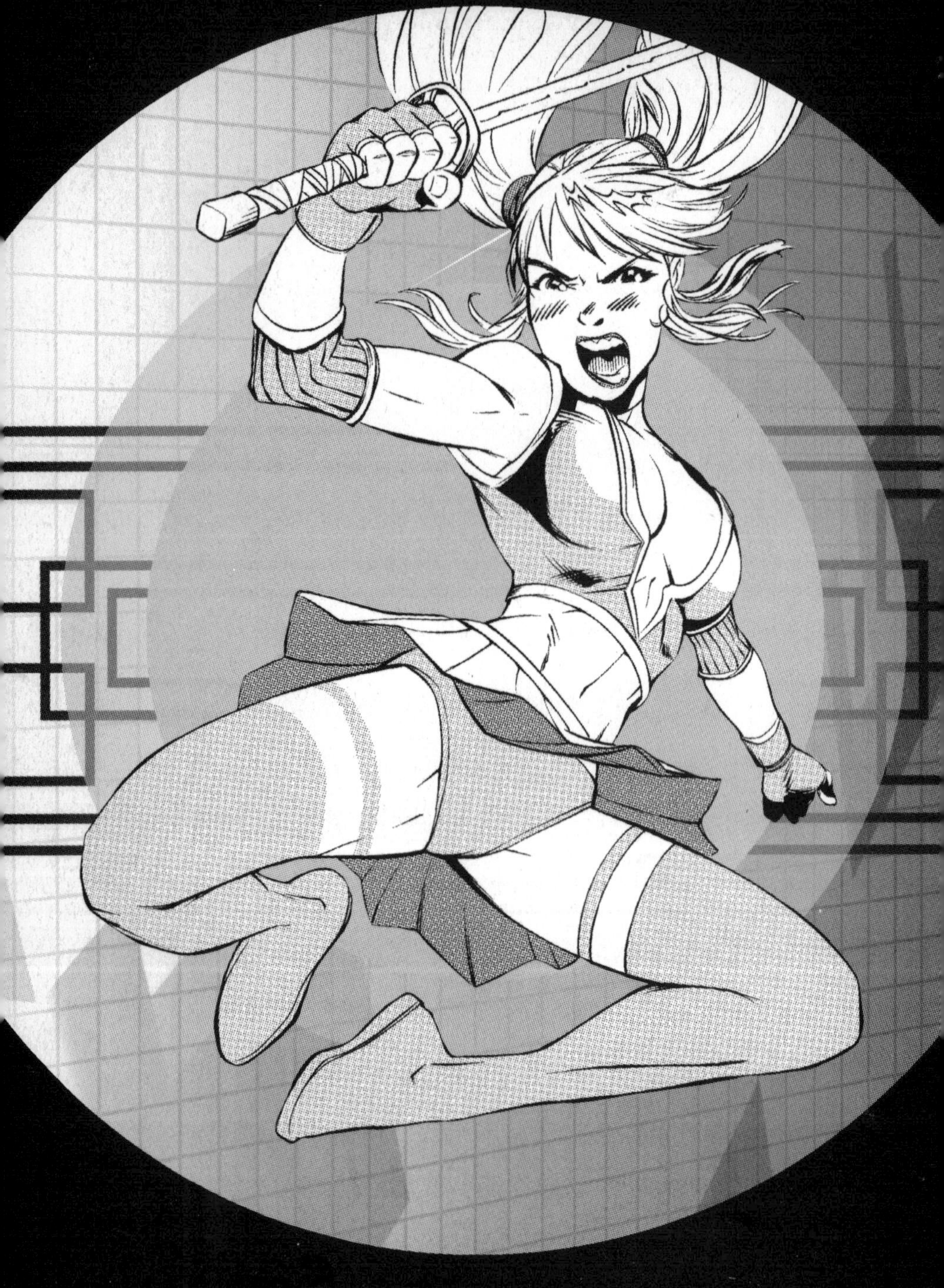

SPYBOY™
THE M★A★N★G★A AFFAIR

SCRIPT
PETER DAVID

PENCILS
POP MHAN

INKS
NORMAN LEE

LETTERS & SHADING
DIGITAL CHAMELEON

COVER ART
POP MHAN

COVER COLOR
DAN JACKSON

DARK HORSE BOOKS™

PUBLISHER
MIKE RICHARDSON

DESIGNER
DEBRA BAILEY

EDITORIAL ASSISTANT
KATIE MOODY

EDITOR
DAVE LAND

SPYBOY™: THE M.A.N.G.A. AFFAIR

This volume collects issues #13.1-13.3 of the Dark Horse comic book series, SpyBoy.

Dark Horse Books™
a division of
Dark Horse Comics, Inc.
10956 SE Main Street
Milwaukie, OR 97222

www.darkhorse.com

To find a comic shop in your area call the
Comic Shop Locator Service toll-free at (888) 266-4226

First edition: November 2003
ISBN: 1-56971-984-5

1 3 5 7 9 10 8 6 4 2

Printed in Canada

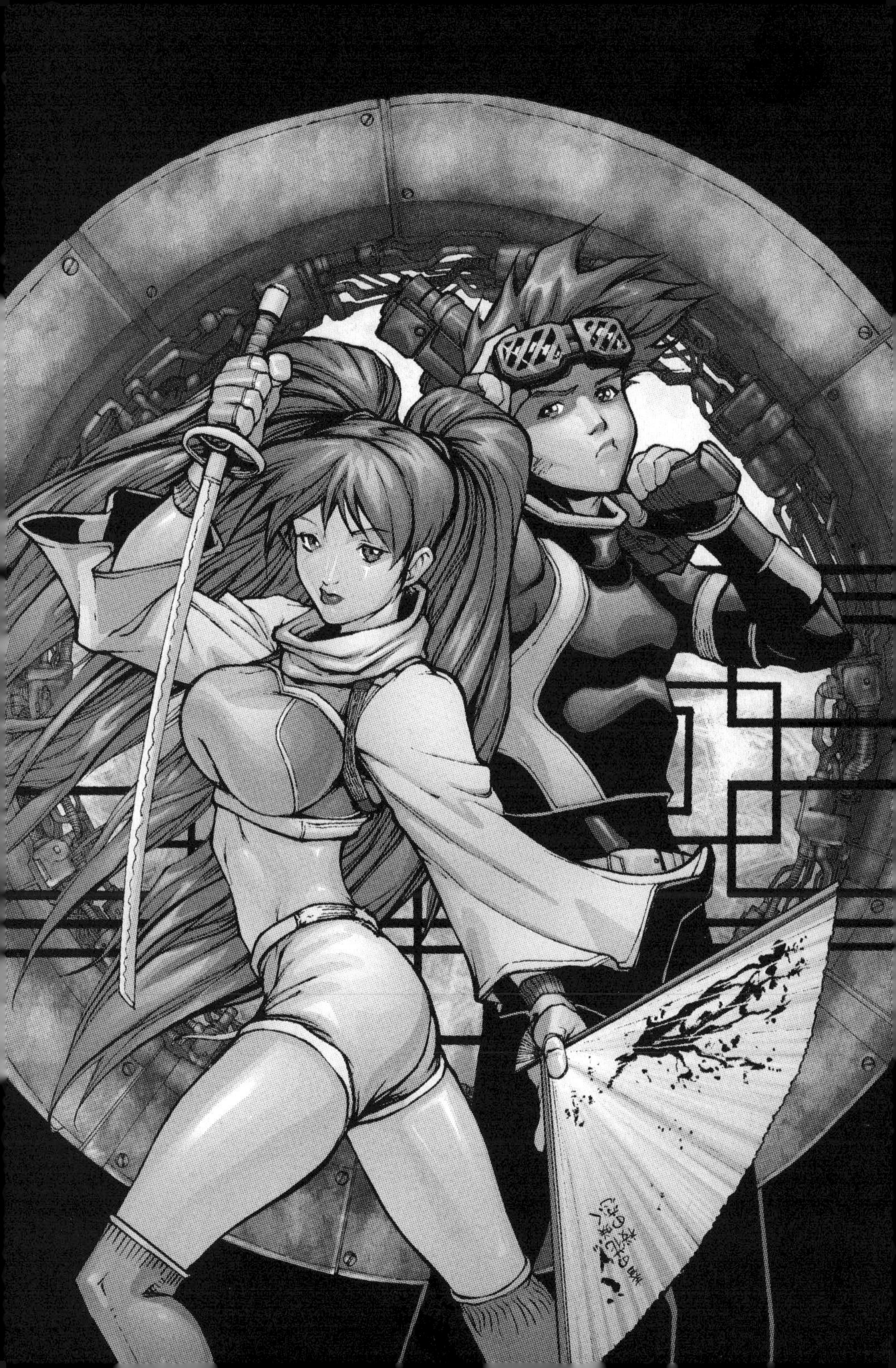

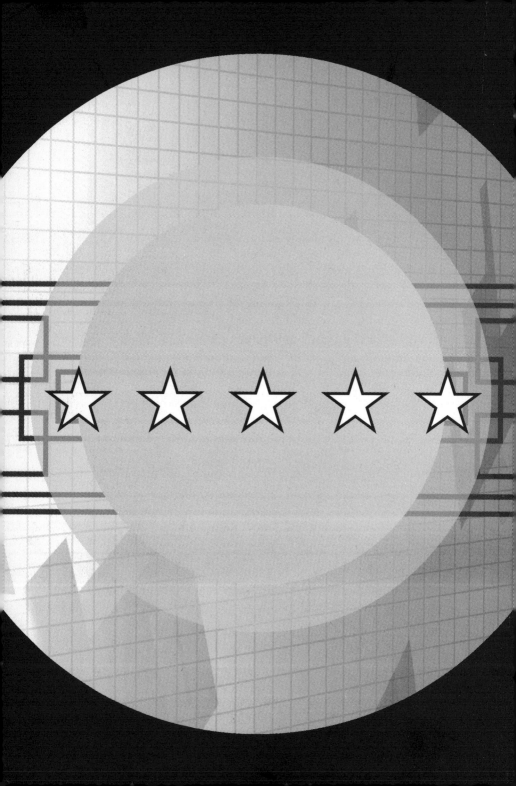

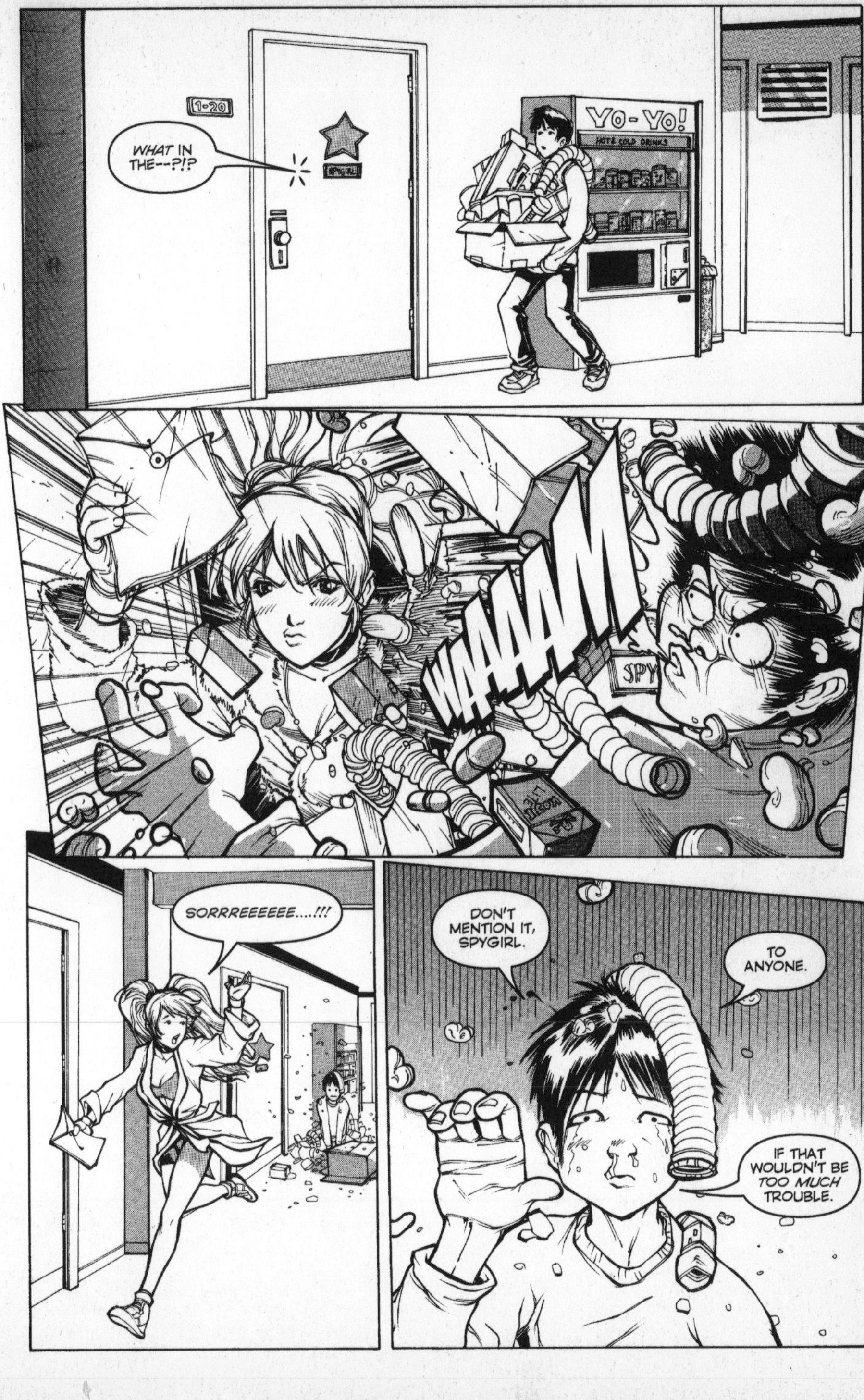
1-20
WHAT IN THE--?!?
SPYGIRL
YO-YO!
HOT & COLD DRINKS
WAAAAM
SPY
SORRREEEEEE....!!!
DON'T MENTION IT, SPYGIRL.
TO ANYONE.
IF THAT WOULDN'T BE *TOO MUCH* TROUBLE.

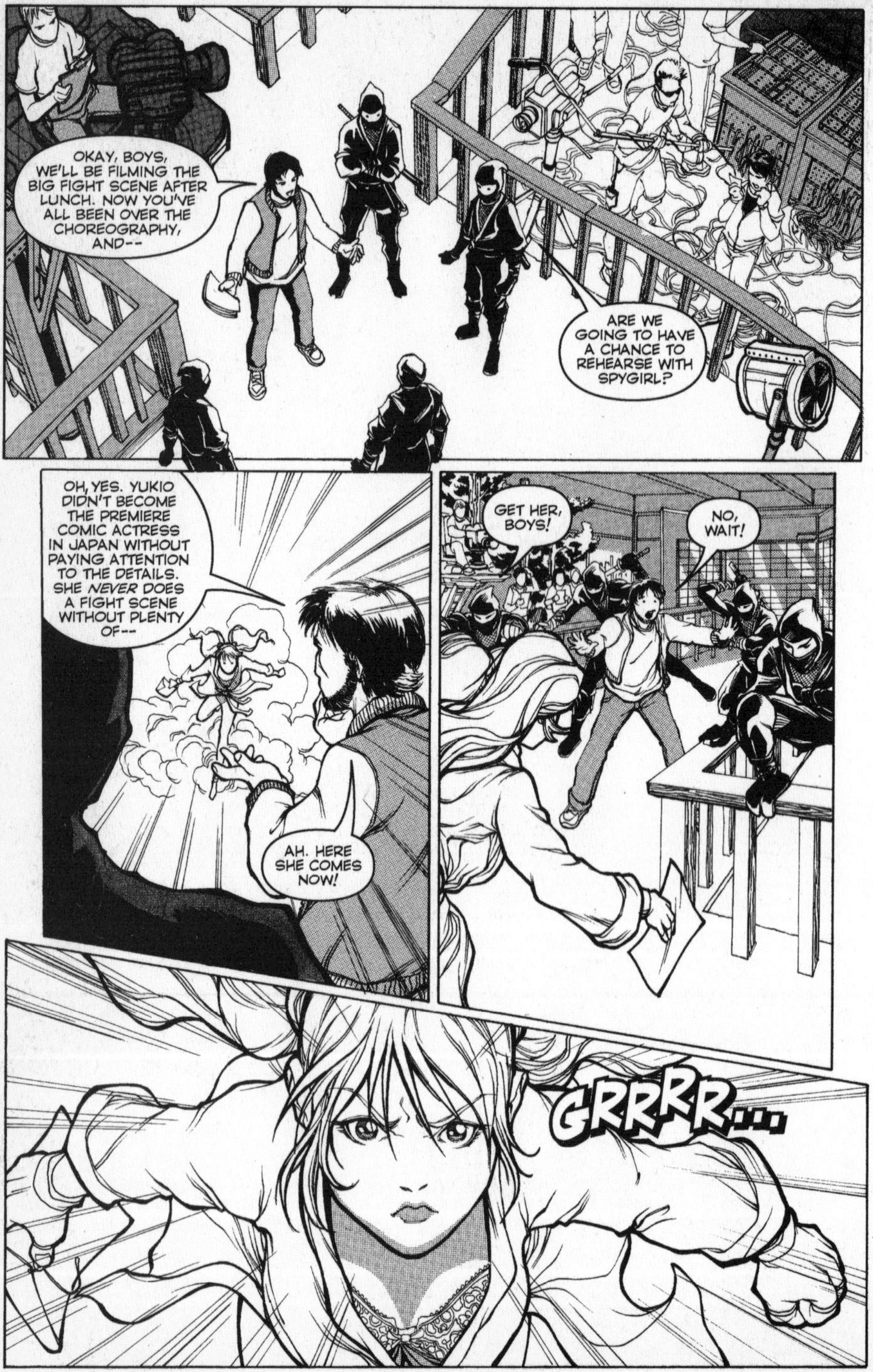
OKAY, BOYS, WE'LL BE FILMING THE BIG FIGHT SCENE AFTER LUNCH. NOW YOU'VE ALL BEEN OVER THE CHOREOGRAPHY, AND--
ARE WE GOING TO HAVE A CHANCE TO REHEARSE WITH SPYGIRL?
OH, YES. YUKIO DIDN'T BECOME THE PREMIERE COMIC ACTRESS IN JAPAN WITHOUT PAYING ATTENTION TO THE DETAILS. SHE *NEVER* DOES A FIGHT SCENE WITHOUT PLENTY OF--
AH. HERE SHE COMES NOW!
GET HER, BOYS!
NO, WAIT!
GRRRR...

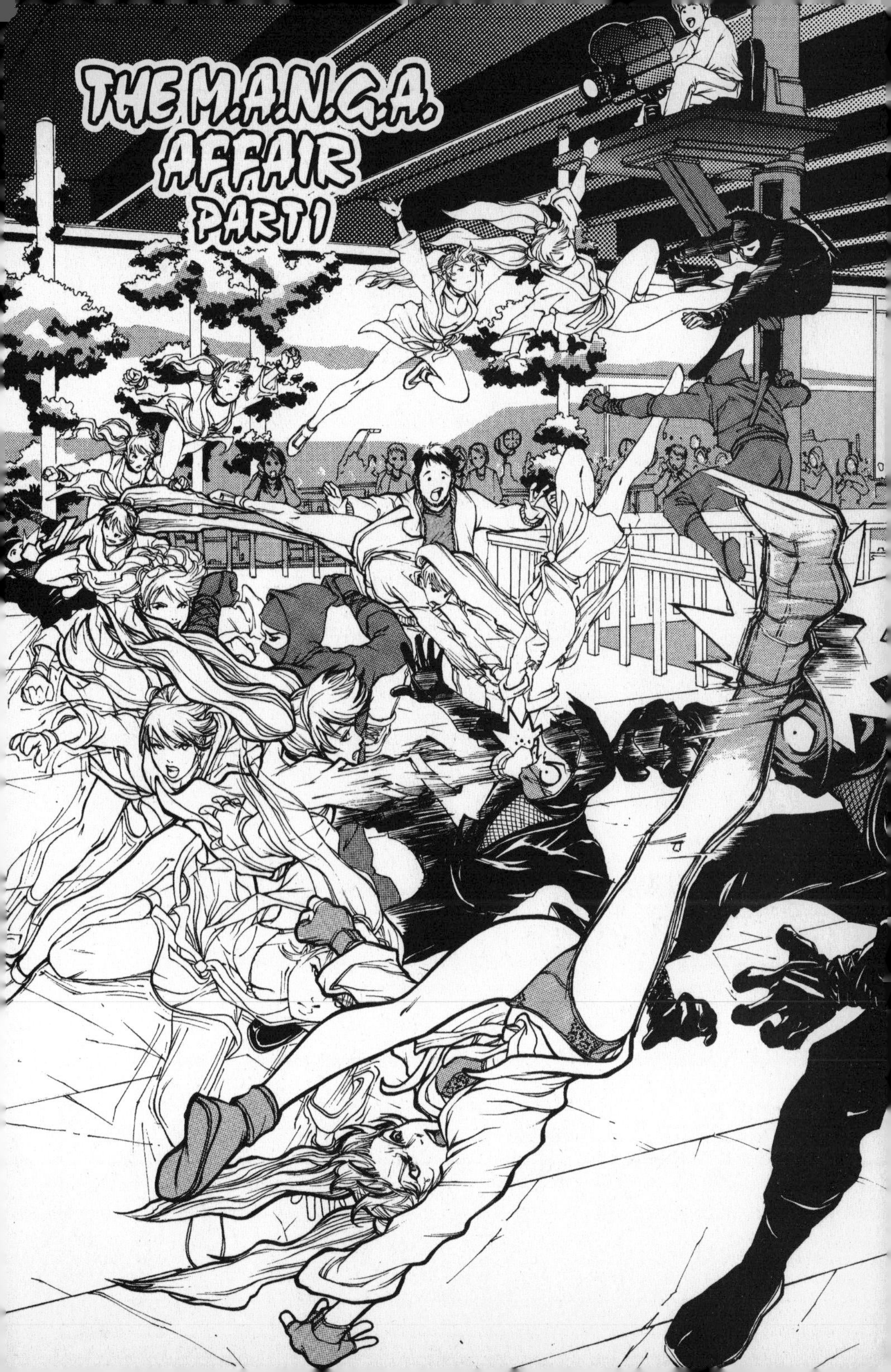
THE M.A.N.G.A.
AFFAIR
PART 1

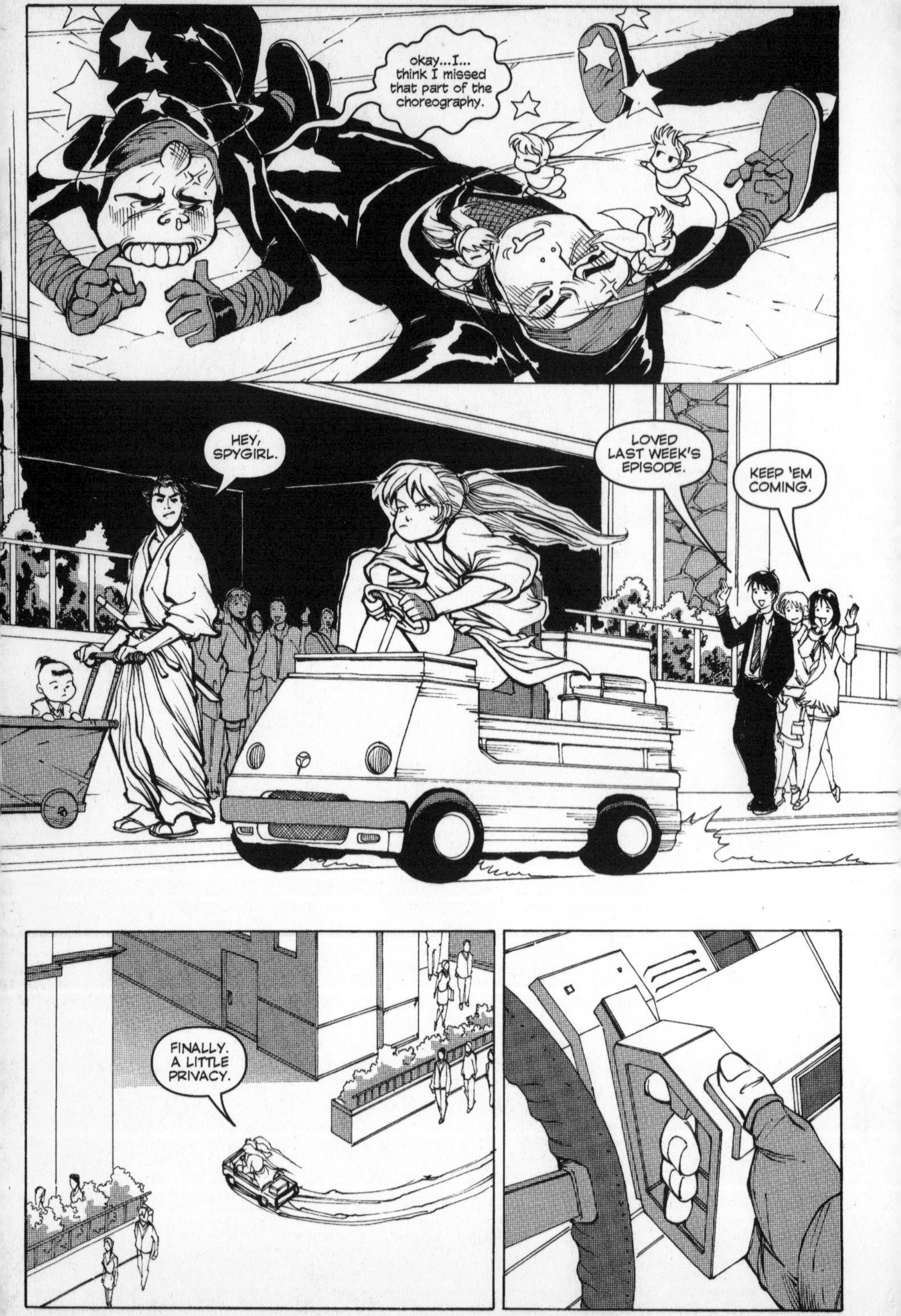
okay...I... think I missed that part of the choreography.
HEY, SPYGIRL.
LOVED LAST WEEK'S EPISODE.
KEEP 'EM COMING.
FINALLY. A LITTLE PRIVACY.

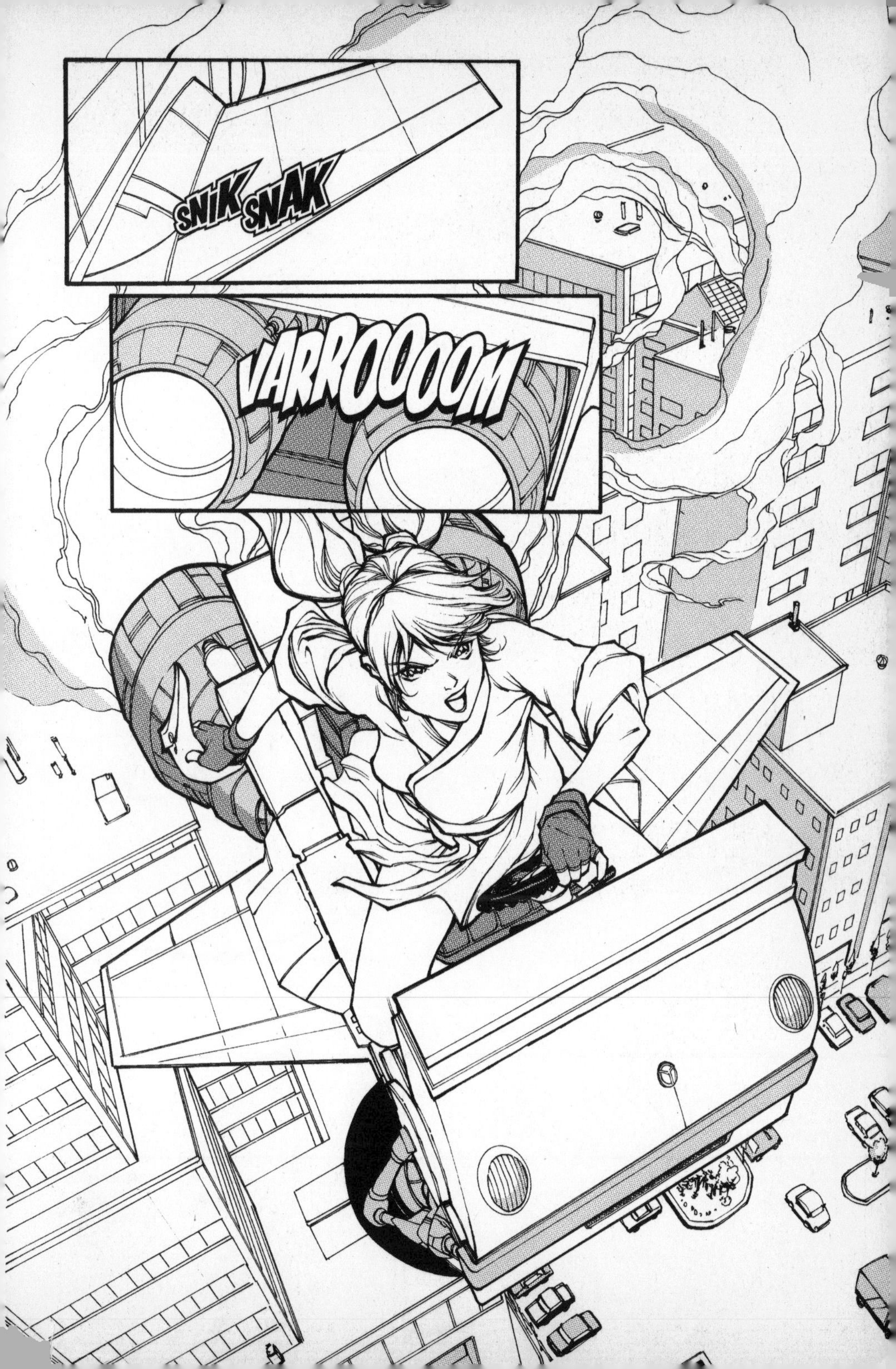
SNIK SNAK
VARROOOOM

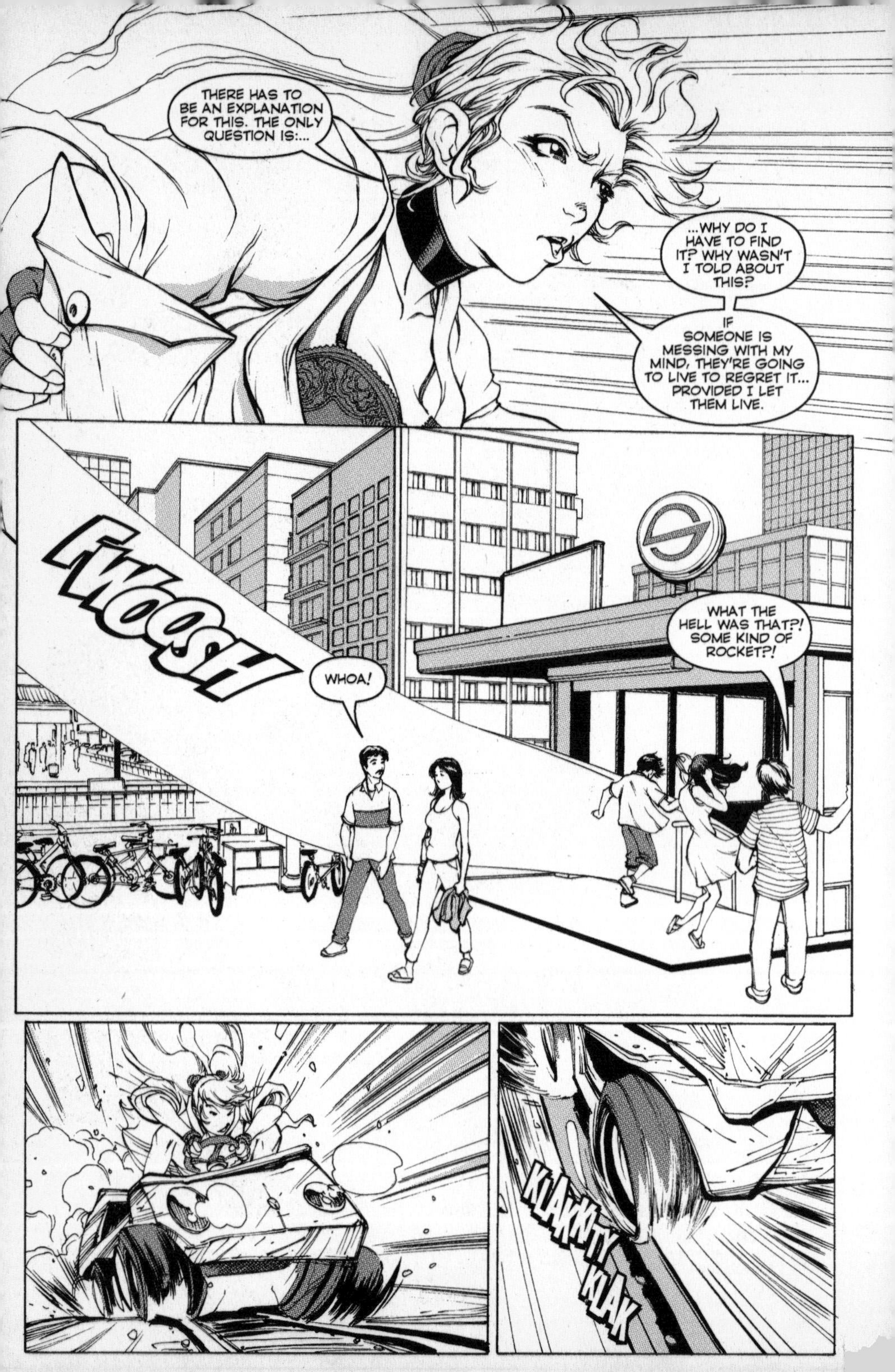
THERE HAS TO BE AN EXPLANATION FOR THIS. THE ONLY QUESTION IS:...
...WHY DO I HAVE TO FIND IT? WHY WASN'T I TOLD ABOUT THIS?
IF SOMEONE IS MESSING WITH MY MIND, THEY'RE GOING TO LIVE TO REGRET IT... PROVIDED I LET THEM LIVE.
FWOOSH
WHOA!
WHAT THE HELL WAS THAT?! SOME KIND OF ROCKET?!
KLAKKITY KLAK

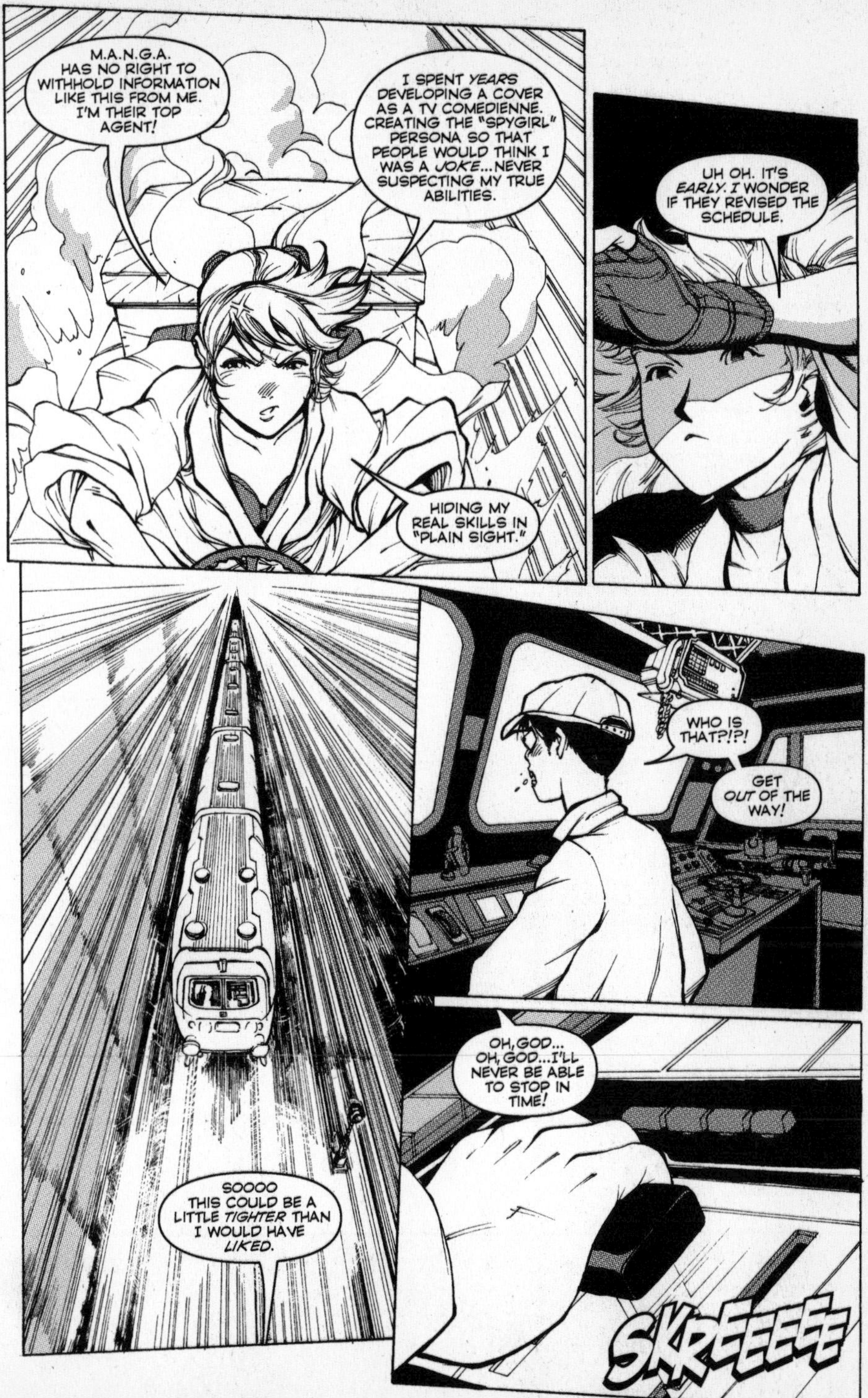
M.A.N.G.A. HAS NO RIGHT TO WITHHOLD INFORMATION LIKE THIS FROM ME. I'M THEIR TOP AGENT!
I SPENT YEARS DEVELOPING A COVER AS A TV COMEDIENNE. CREATING THE "SPYGIRL" PERSONA SO THAT PEOPLE WOULD THINK I WAS A JOKE...NEVER SUSPECTING MY TRUE ABILITIES.
HIDING MY REAL SKILLS IN "PLAIN SIGHT."
UH OH. IT'S EARLY. I WONDER IF THEY REVISED THE SCHEDULE.
SOOOO THIS COULD BE A LITTLE TIGHTER THAN I WOULD HAVE LIKED.
WHO IS THAT?!?!
GET OUT OF THE WAY!
OH, GOD... OH, GOD...I'LL NEVER BE ABLE TO STOP IN TIME!
SKREEEEEE

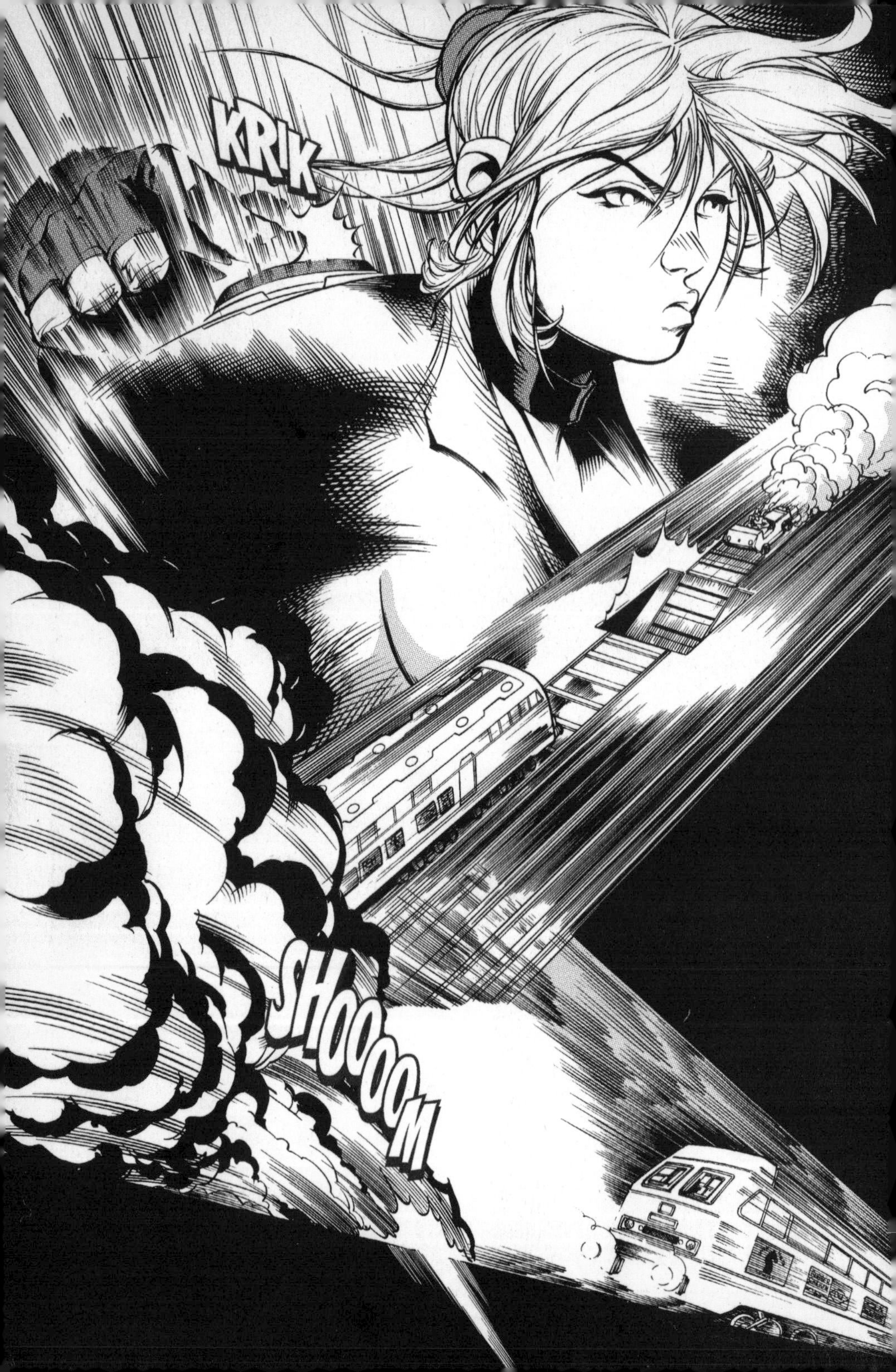
KRIK
SHOOOOM

<WHY DID THE HONORABLE ENGINEER HIT THE BRAKE?>

<UNKNOWN. FORTUNATELY, WE'RE PACKED IN HERE SO TIGHTLY, WE CAN'T BE THROWN AROUND.>*

SKREE

*ACTUAL JAPANESE DIALOGUE CONTAINS FAR MORE PROFANITY. TRANSLATION HAS BEEN SOFTENED FOR GENERAL AUDIENCES. THANK YOU. —YOUR PALS AT DARK HORSE.

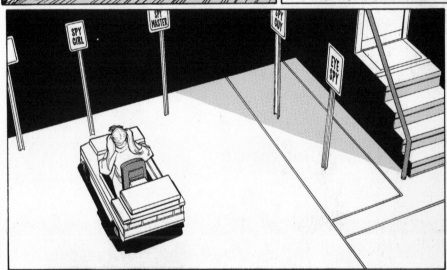

SPY GIRL

SPY MASTER

SPY GUY

EYE SPY

SPY GIRL

NOW... WE'LL SEE WHAT MR. LI HAS TO SAY ABOUT THIS.

SPY GIRL

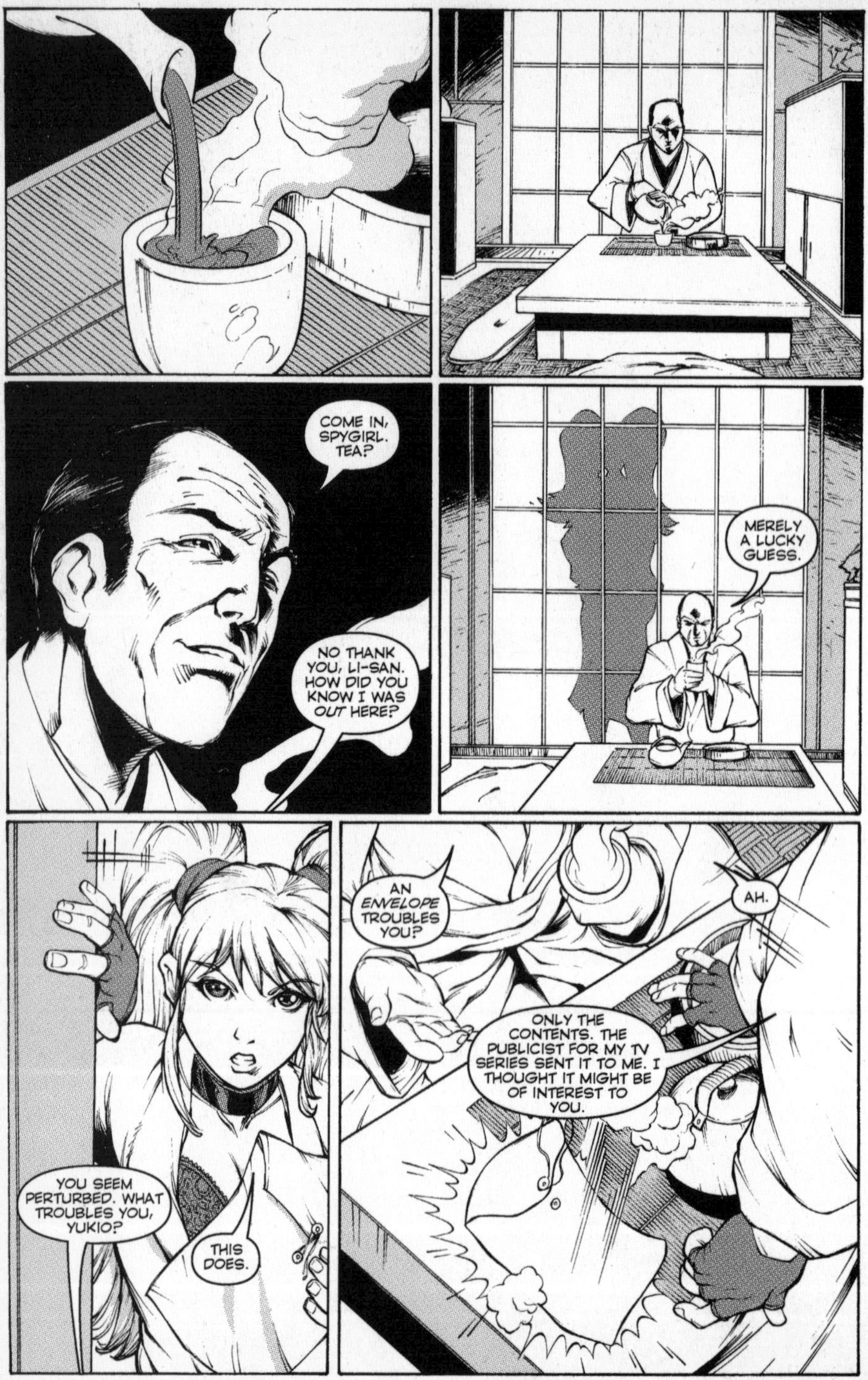
COME IN, SPYGIRL. TEA?
NO THANK YOU, LI-SAN. HOW DID YOU KNOW I WAS *OUT* HERE?
MERELY A LUCKY GUESS.
YOU SEEM PERTURBED. WHAT TROUBLES YOU, YUKIO?
THIS DOES.
AN *ENVELOPE* TROUBLES YOU?
AH.
ONLY THE CONTENTS. THE PUBLICIST FOR MY TV SERIES SENT IT TO ME. I THOUGHT IT MIGHT BE OF INTEREST TO YOU.

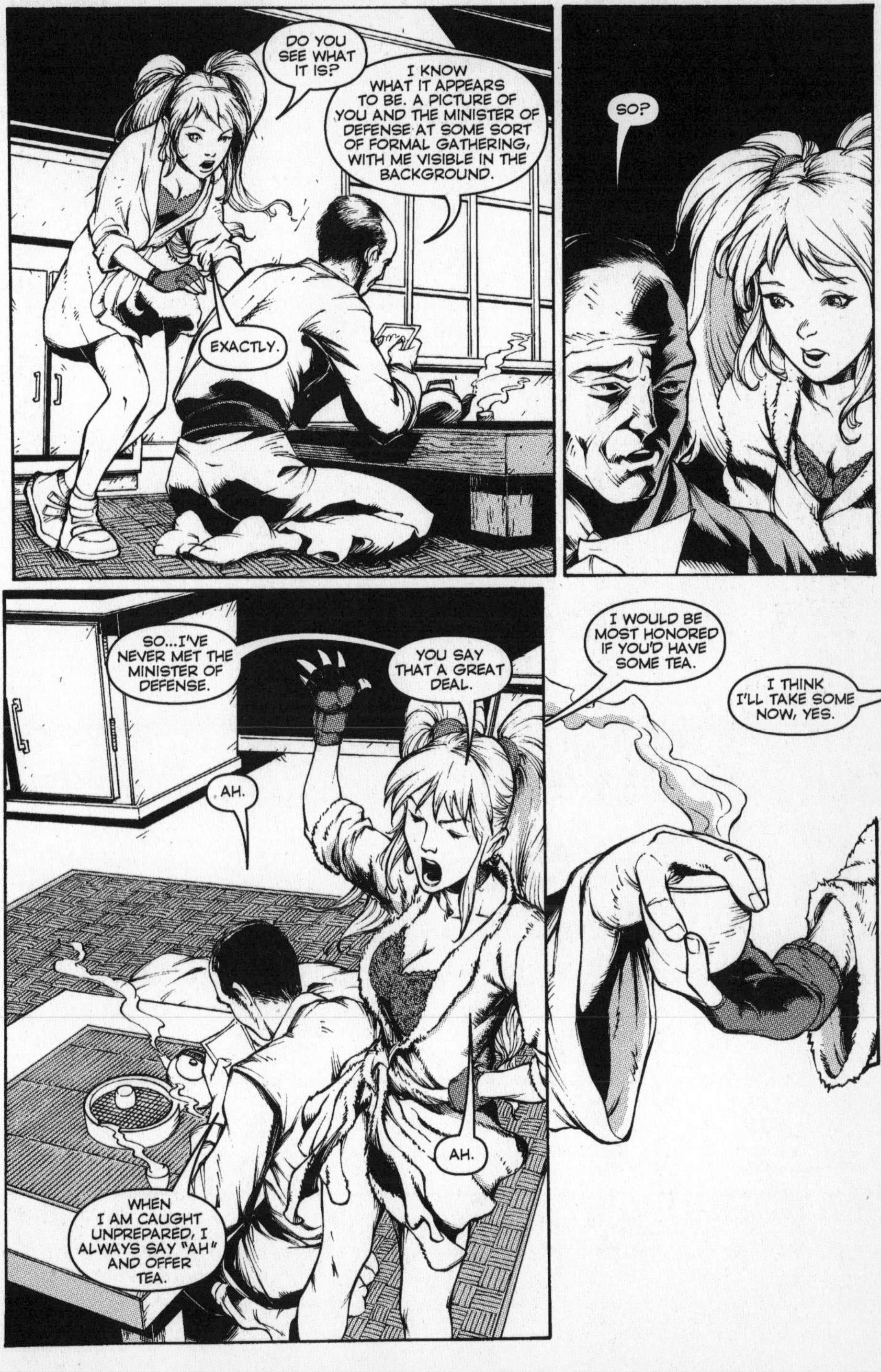
DO YOU SEE WHAT IT IS?
I KNOW WHAT IT APPEARS TO BE. A PICTURE OF YOU AND THE MINISTER OF DEFENSE AT SOME SORT OF FORMAL GATHERING, WITH ME VISIBLE IN THE BACKGROUND.
EXACTLY.
SO?
SO...I'VE NEVER MET THE MINISTER OF DEFENSE.
YOU SAY THAT A GREAT DEAL.
AH.
I WOULD BE MOST HONORED IF YOU'D HAVE SOME TEA.
I THINK I'LL TAKE SOME NOW, YES.
AH.
WHEN I AM CAUGHT UNPREPARED, I ALWAYS SAY "AH" AND OFFER TEA.

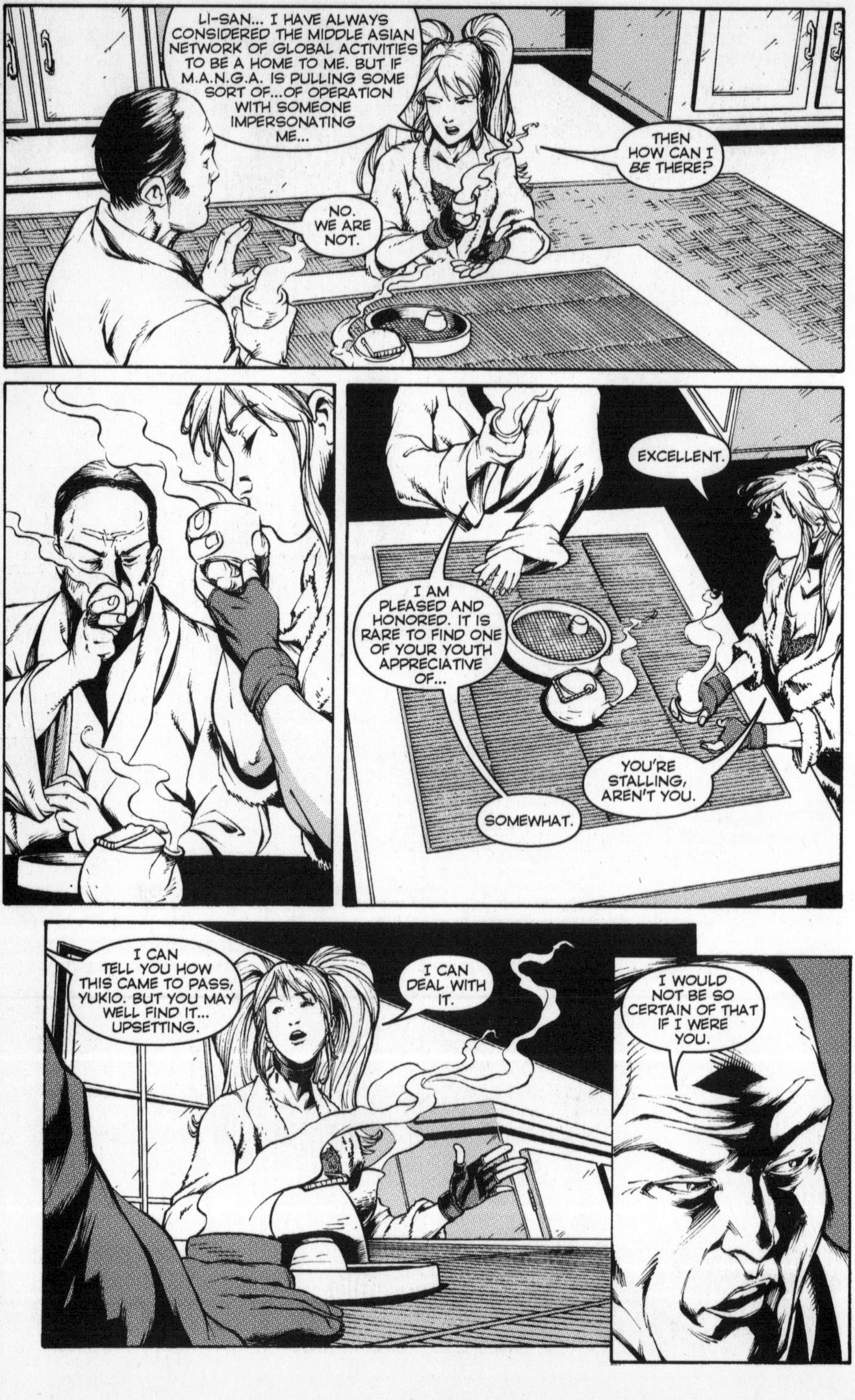
LI-SAN... I HAVE ALWAYS CONSIDERED THE MIDDLE ASIAN NETWORK OF GLOBAL ACTIVITIES TO BE A HOME TO ME. BUT IF M.A.N.G.A. IS PULLING SOME SORT OF...OF OPERATION WITH SOMEONE IMPERSONATING ME...
NO. WE ARE NOT.
THEN HOW CAN I BE THERE?
EXCELLENT.
I AM PLEASED AND HONORED. IT IS RARE TO FIND ONE OF YOUR YOUTH APPRECIATIVE OF...
YOU'RE STALLING, AREN'T YOU.
SOMEWHAT.
I CAN TELL YOU HOW THIS CAME TO PASS, YUKIO. BUT YOU MAY WELL FIND IT... UPSETTING.
I CAN DEAL WITH IT.
I WOULD NOT BE SO CERTAIN OF THAT IF I WERE YOU.

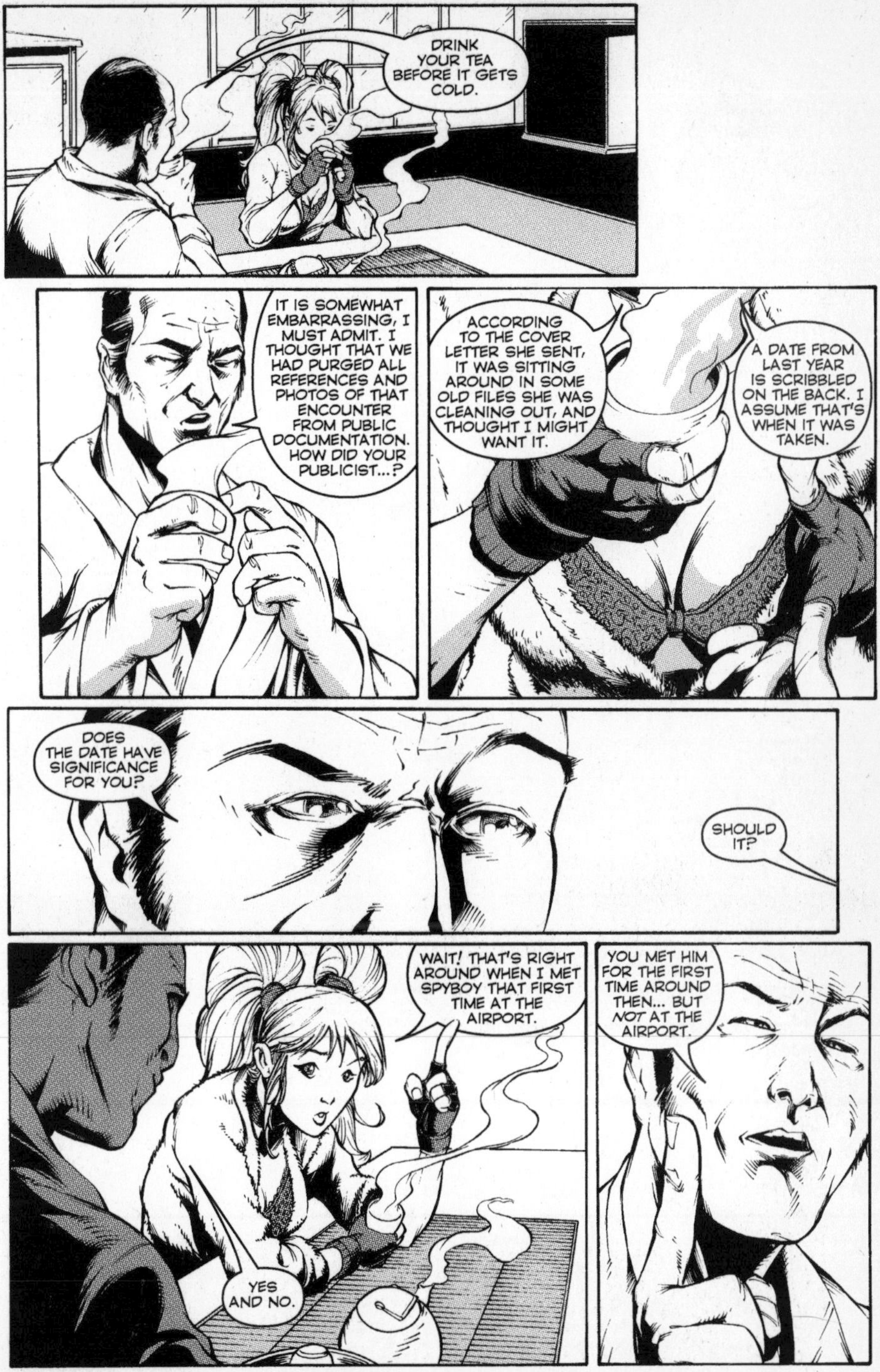
DRINK YOUR TEA BEFORE IT GETS COLD.
IT IS SOMEWHAT EMBARRASSING, I MUST ADMIT. I THOUGHT THAT WE HAD PURGED ALL REFERENCES AND PHOTOS OF THAT ENCOUNTER FROM PUBLIC DOCUMENTATION. HOW DID YOUR PUBLICIST...?
ACCORDING TO THE COVER LETTER SHE SENT, IT WAS SITTING AROUND IN SOME OLD FILES SHE WAS CLEANING OUT, AND THOUGHT I MIGHT WANT IT.
A DATE FROM LAST YEAR IS SCRIBBLED ON THE BACK. I ASSUME THAT'S WHEN IT WAS TAKEN.
DOES THE DATE HAVE SIGNIFICANCE FOR YOU?
SHOULD IT?
WAIT! THAT'S RIGHT AROUND WHEN I MET SPYBOY THAT FIRST TIME AT THE AIRPORT.
YES AND NO.
YOU MET HIM FOR THE FIRST TIME AROUND THEN... BUT *NOT* AT THE AIRPORT.

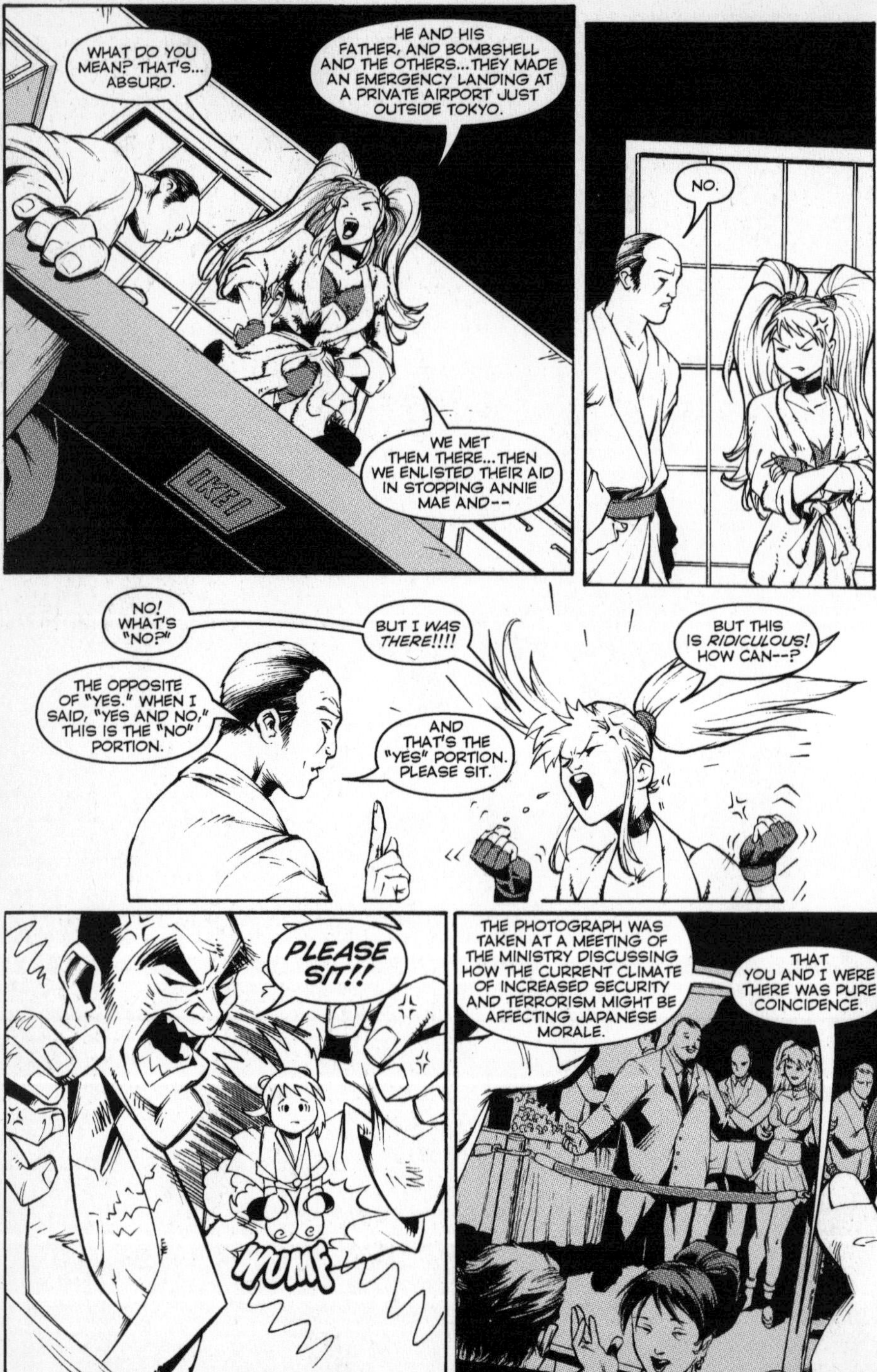
WHAT DO YOU MEAN? THAT'S... ABSURD.
HE AND HIS FATHER, AND BOMBSHELL AND THE OTHERS...THEY MADE AN EMERGENCY LANDING AT A PRIVATE AIRPORT JUST OUTSIDE TOKYO.
WE MET THEM THERE...THEN WE ENLISTED THEIR AID IN STOPPING ANNIE MAE AND--
NO.
NO! WHAT'S "NO?"
BUT I *WAS THERE*!!!!
BUT THIS IS *RIDICULOUS*! HOW CAN--?
THE OPPOSITE OF "YES." WHEN I SAID, "YES AND NO," THIS IS THE "NO" PORTION.
AND THAT'S THE "YES" PORTION. PLEASE SIT.
PLEASE SIT!!
WUMF
THE PHOTOGRAPH WAS TAKEN AT A MEETING OF THE MINISTRY DISCUSSING HOW THE CURRENT CLIMATE OF INCREASED SECURITY AND TERRORISM MIGHT BE AFFECTING JAPANESE MORALE.
THAT YOU AND I WERE THERE WAS PURE COINCIDENCE.

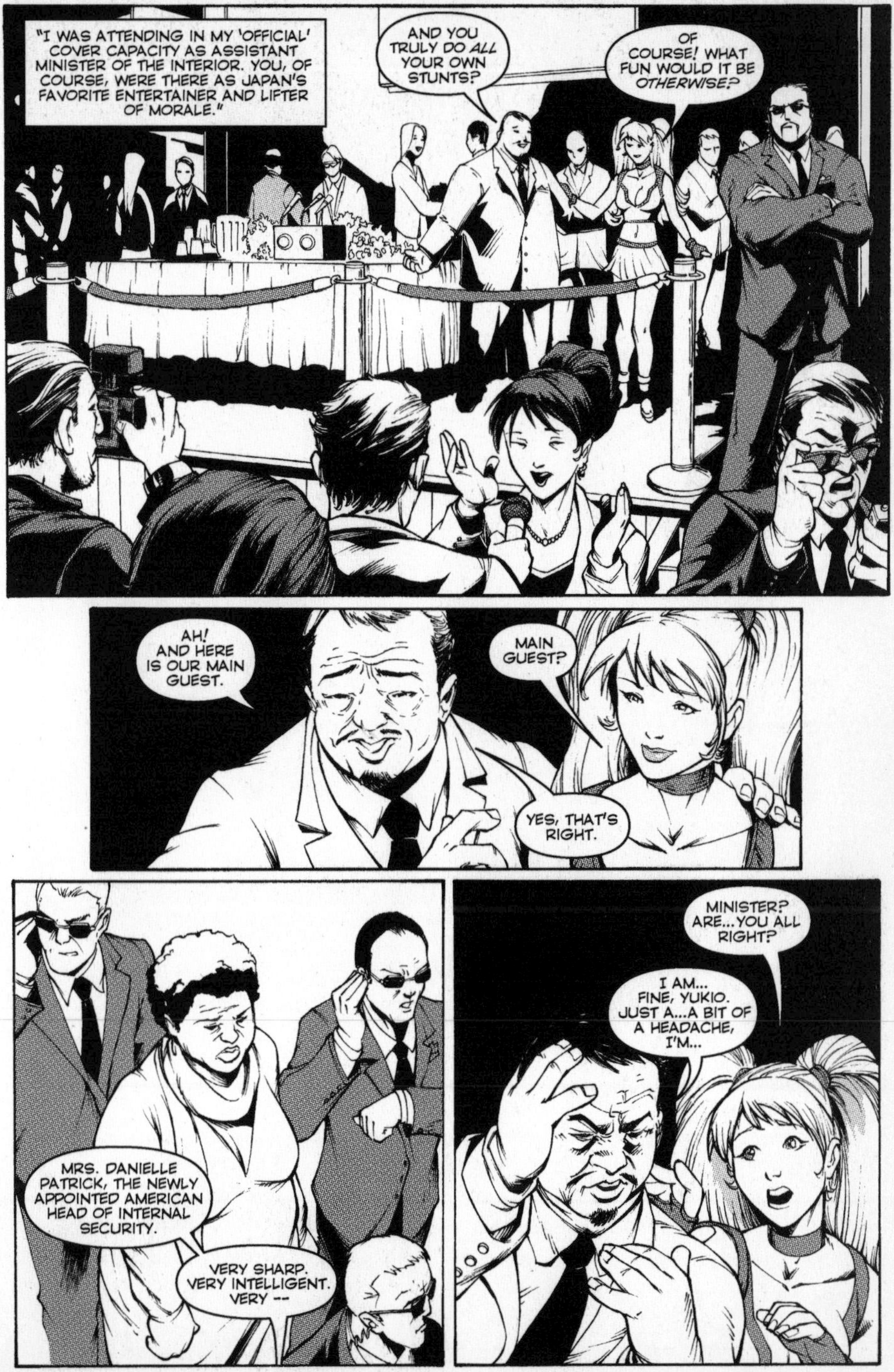
"I WAS ATTENDING IN MY 'OFFICIAL' COVER CAPACITY AS ASSISTANT MINISTER OF THE INTERIOR. YOU, OF COURSE, WERE THERE AS JAPAN'S FAVORITE ENTERTAINER AND LIFTER OF MORALE."
AND YOU TRULY DO *ALL* YOUR OWN STUNTS?
OF COURSE! WHAT FUN WOULD IT BE *OTHERWISE?*
AH! AND HERE IS OUR MAIN GUEST.
MAIN GUEST?
YES, THAT'S RIGHT.
MRS. DANIELLE PATRICK, THE NEWLY APPOINTED AMERICAN HEAD OF INTERNAL SECURITY.
VERY SHARP. VERY INTELLIGENT. VERY --
MINISTER? ARE...YOU ALL RIGHT?
I AM... FINE, YUKIO. JUST A...A BIT OF A HEADACHE, I'M...

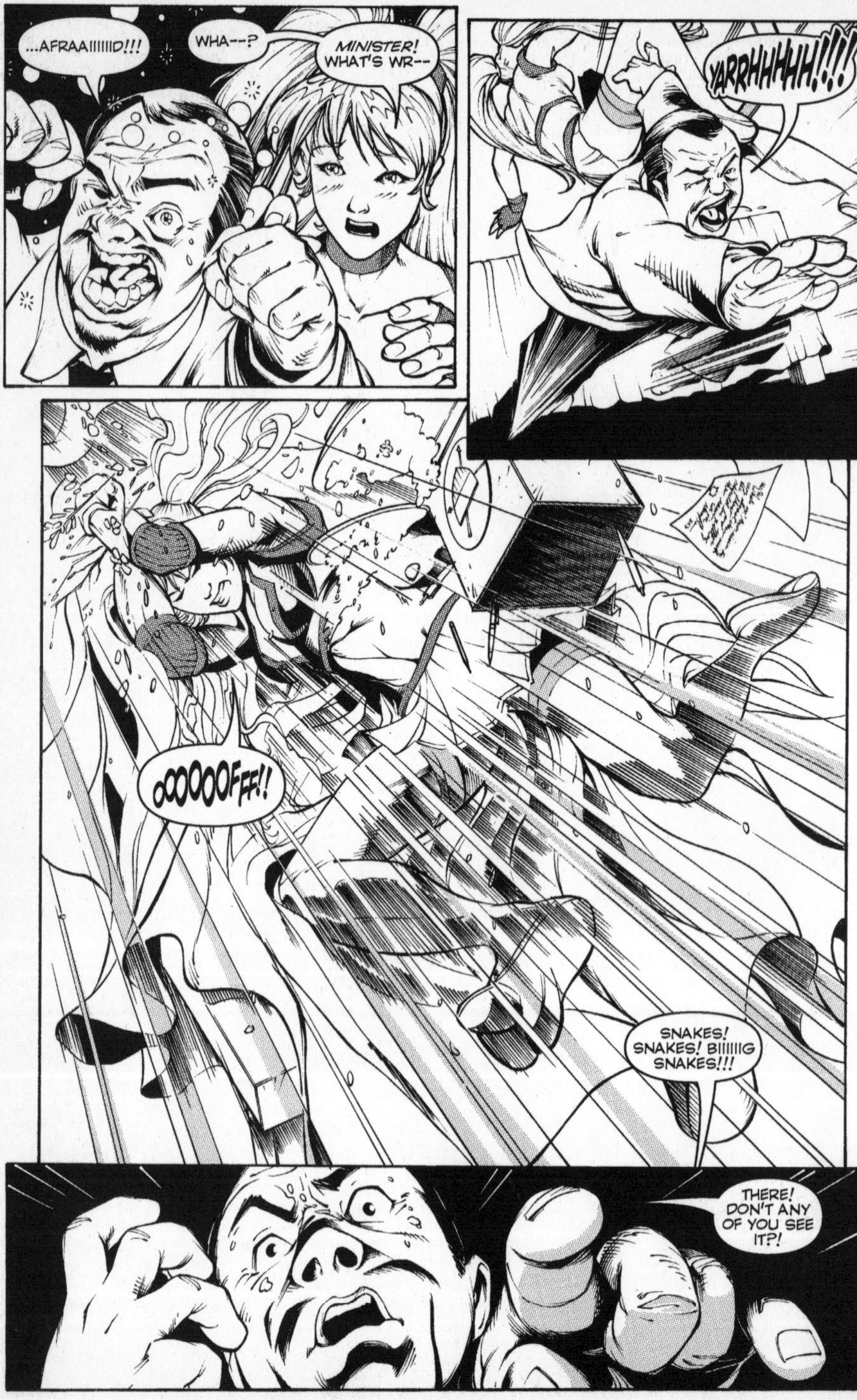
...AFRAAIIIIIID!!!
WHA--?
MINISTER! WHAT'S WR--
YARRHHHHH!!!!
OOOOOOFFF!!
SNAKES! SNAKES! BIIIIIIG SNAKES!!!
THERE! DON'T ANY OF YOU SEE IT?!

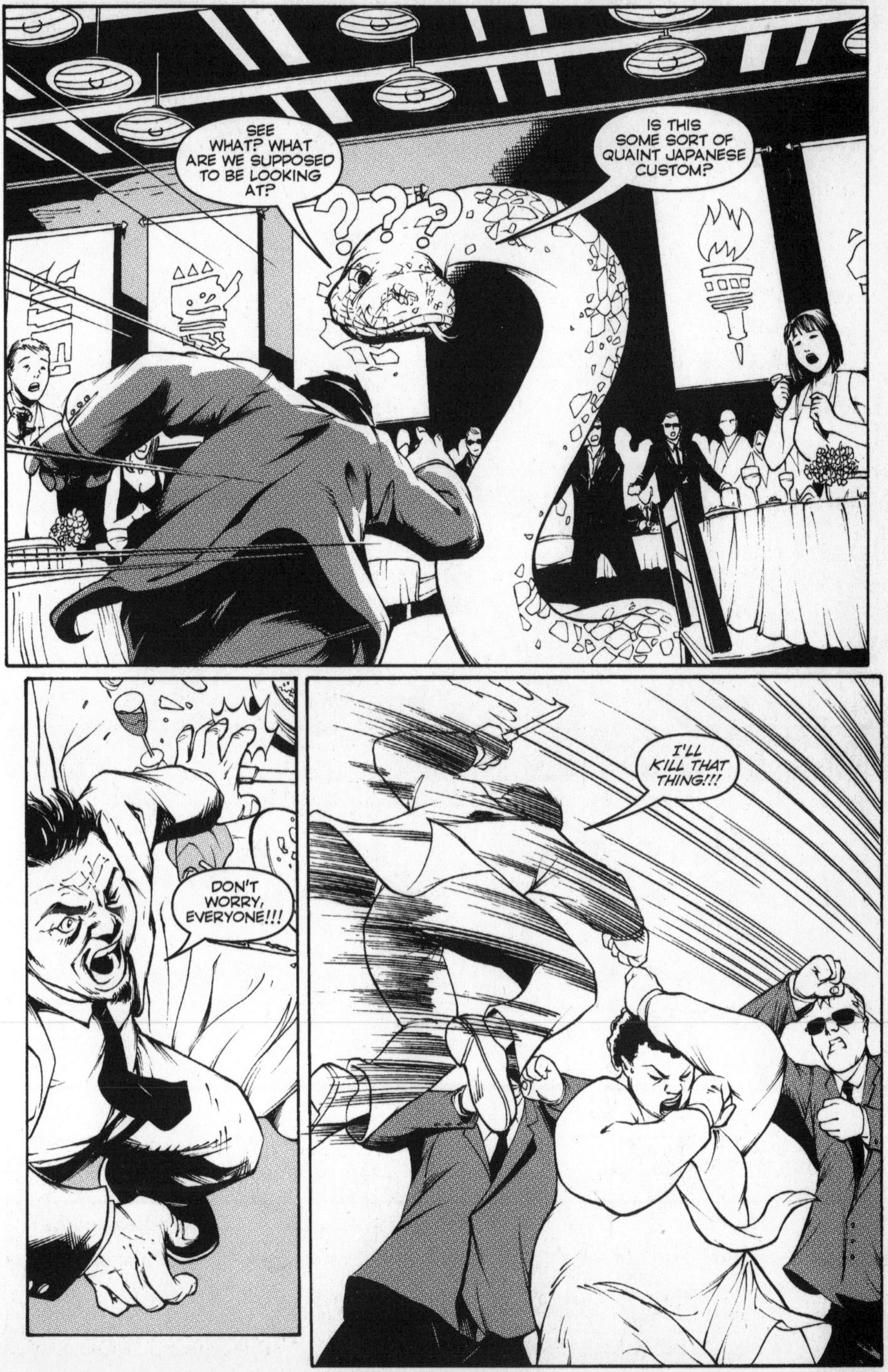
SEE WHAT? WHAT ARE WE SUPPOSED TO BE LOOKING AT?
IS THIS SOME SORT OF QUAINT JAPANESE CUSTOM?
DON'T WORRY, EVERYONE!!!
I'LL KILL THAT THING!!!

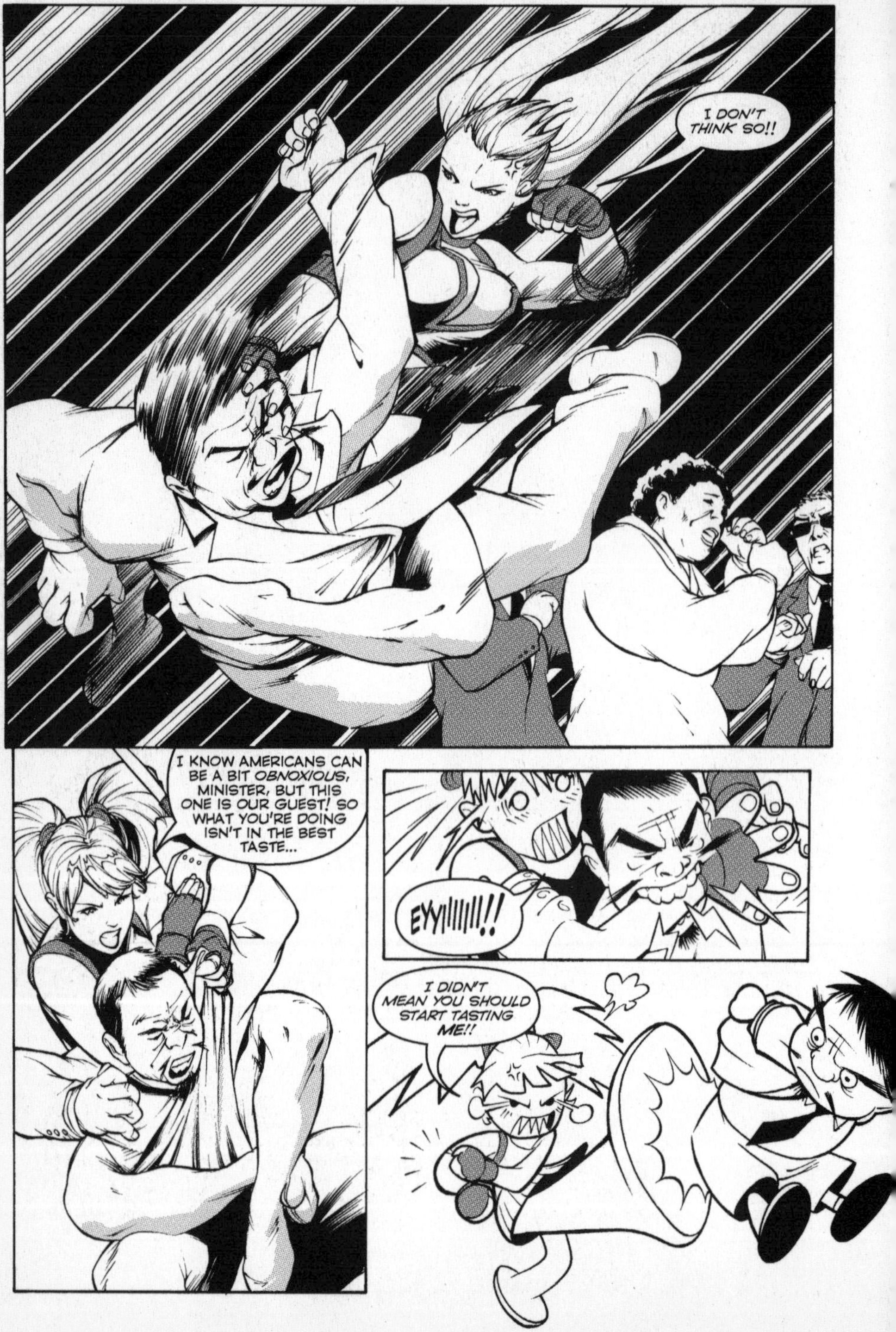
I DON'T THINK SO!!
I KNOW AMERICANS CAN BE A BIT OBNOXIOUS, MINISTER, BUT THIS ONE IS OUR GUEST! SO WHAT YOU'RE DOING ISN'T IN THE BEST TASTE...
EYYIIIIIII!!
I DIDN'T MEAN YOU SHOULD START TASTING ME!!

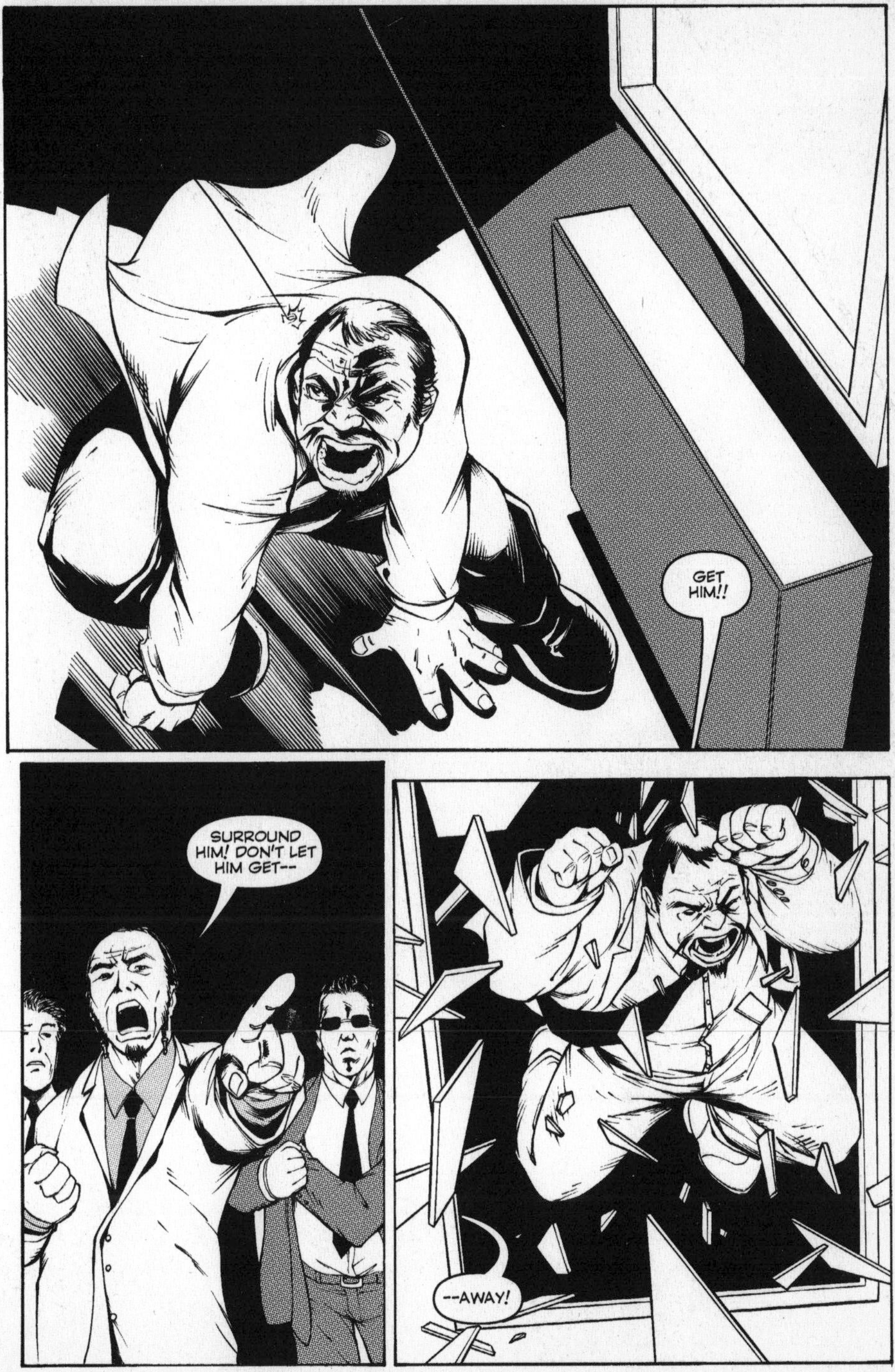
GET HIM!!
SURROUND HIM! DON'T LET HIM GET--
--AWAY!

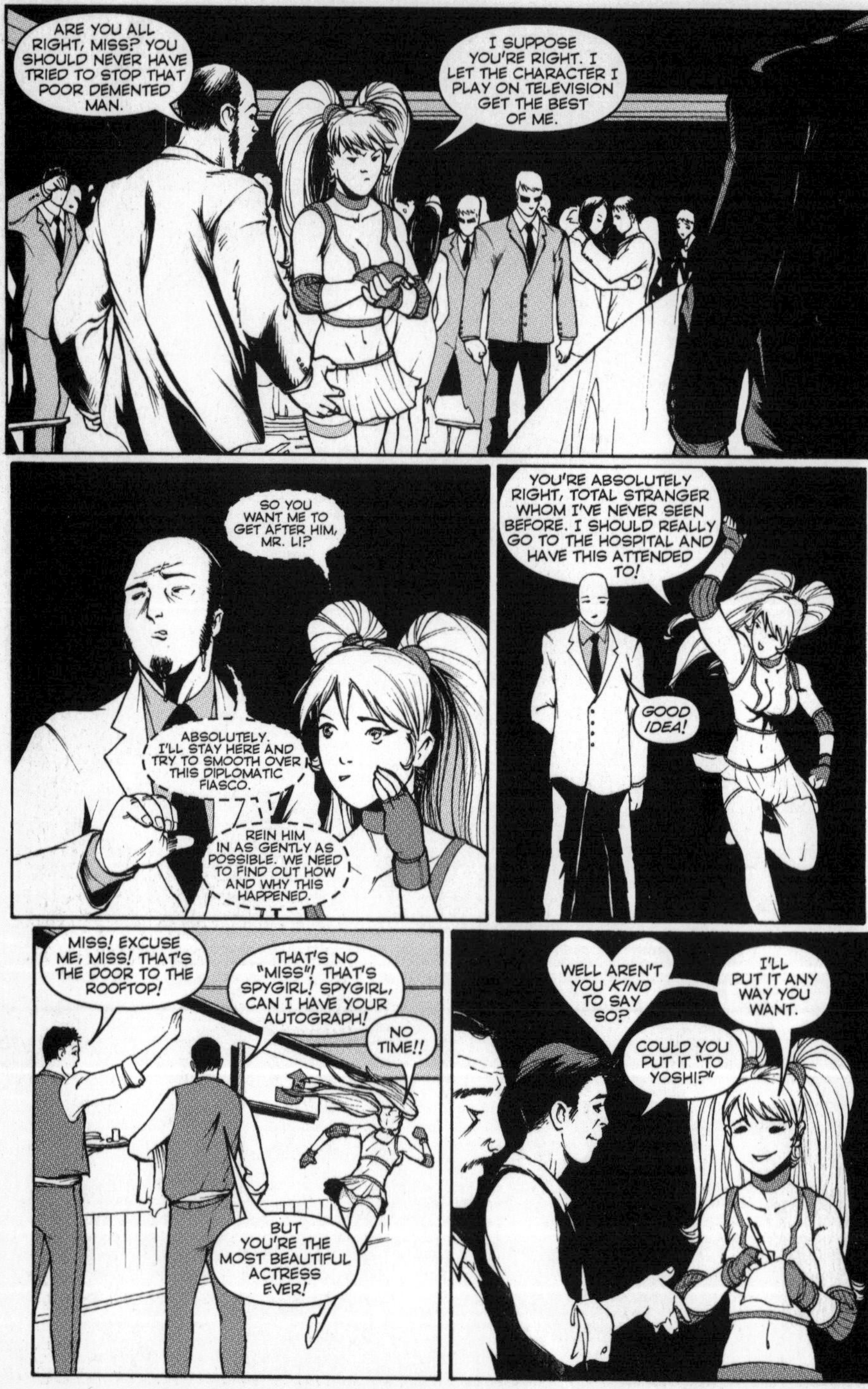
ARE YOU ALL RIGHT, MISS? YOU SHOULD NEVER HAVE TRIED TO STOP THAT POOR DEMENTED MAN.
I SUPPOSE YOU'RE RIGHT. I LET THE CHARACTER I PLAY ON TELEVISION GET THE BEST OF ME.
SO YOU WANT ME TO GET AFTER HIM, MR. LI?
ABSOLUTELY. I'LL STAY HERE AND TRY TO SMOOTH OVER THIS DIPLOMATIC FIASCO.
REIN HIM IN AS GENTLY AS POSSIBLE. WE NEED TO FIND OUT HOW AND WHY THIS HAPPENED.
YOU'RE ABSOLUTELY RIGHT, TOTAL STRANGER WHOM I'VE NEVER SEEN BEFORE. I SHOULD REALLY GO TO THE HOSPITAL AND HAVE THIS ATTENDED TO!
GOOD IDEA!
MISS! EXCUSE ME, MISS! THAT'S THE DOOR TO THE ROOFTOP!
THAT'S NO "MISS"! THAT'S SPYGIRL! SPYGIRL, CAN I HAVE YOUR AUTOGRAPH!
NO TIME!!
BUT YOU'RE THE MOST BEAUTIFUL ACTRESS EVER!
WELL AREN'T YOU *KIND* TO SAY SO?
I'LL PUT IT ANY WAY YOU WANT.
COULD YOU PUT IT "TO YOSHI?"

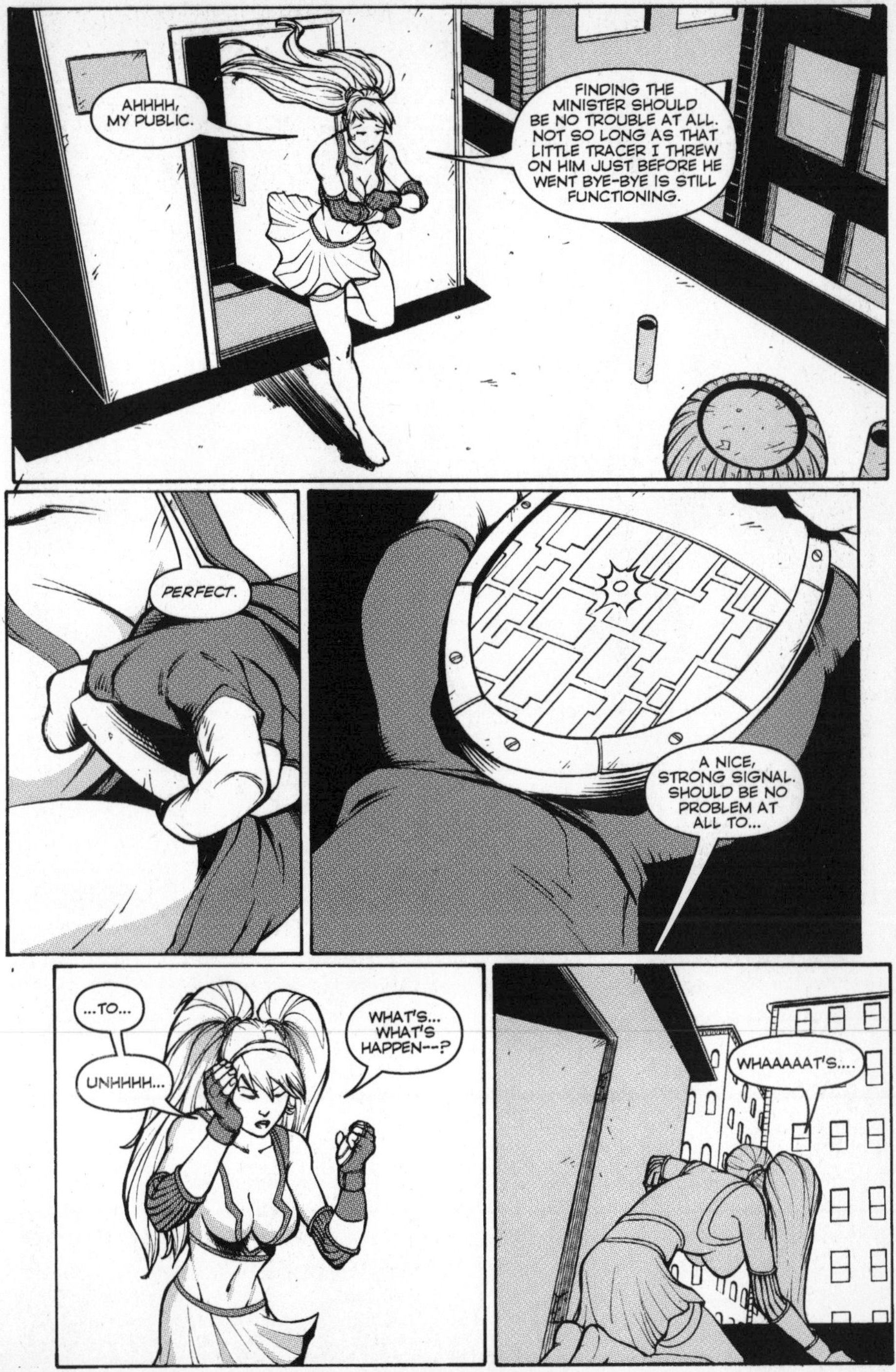
AHHHH, MY PUBLIC.
FINDING THE MINISTER SHOULD BE NO TROUBLE AT ALL. NOT SO LONG AS THAT LITTLE TRACER I THREW ON HIM JUST BEFORE HE WENT BYE-BYE IS STILL FUNCTIONING.
PERFECT.
A NICE, STRONG SIGNAL. SHOULD BE NO PROBLEM AT ALL TO...
...TO...
UNHHHH...
WHAT'S... WHAT'S HAPPEN--?
WHAAAAAT'S....

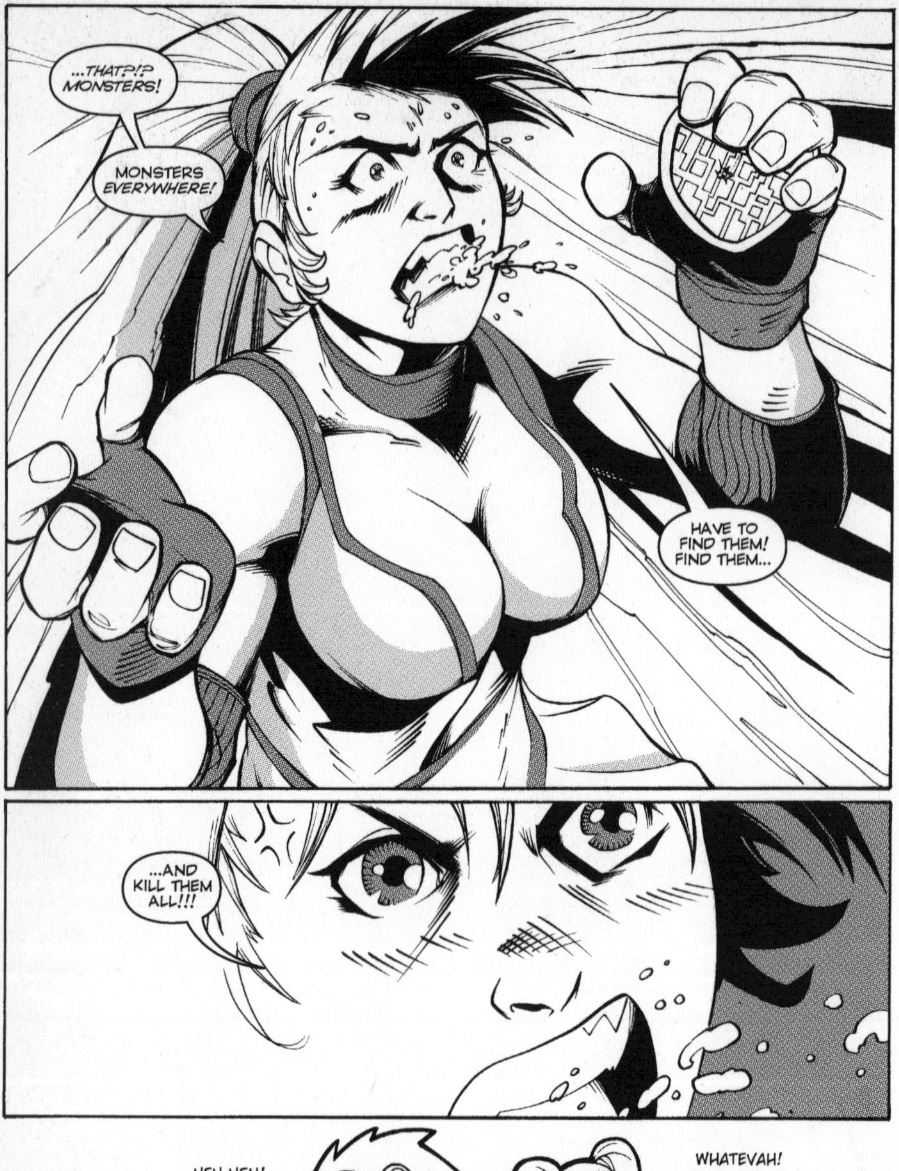
...THAT?!? MONSTERS!
MONSTERS EVERYWHERE!
HAVE TO FIND THEM! FIND THEM...
...AND KILL THEM ALL!!!

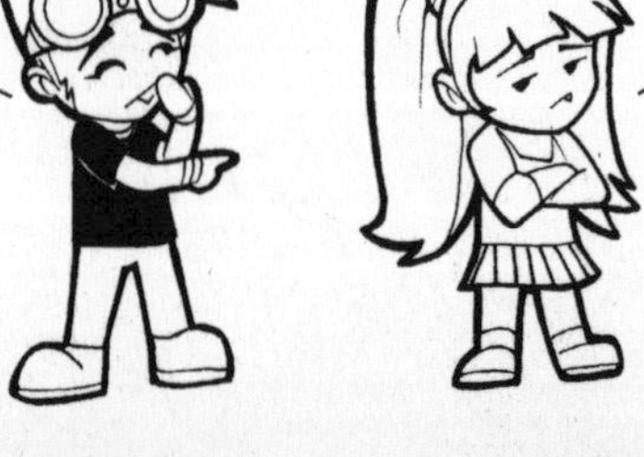
HEH HEH! YOU GOT BRAINWASHED!
WHATEVAH! YOU WEREN'T EVEN IN THIS ISSUE...

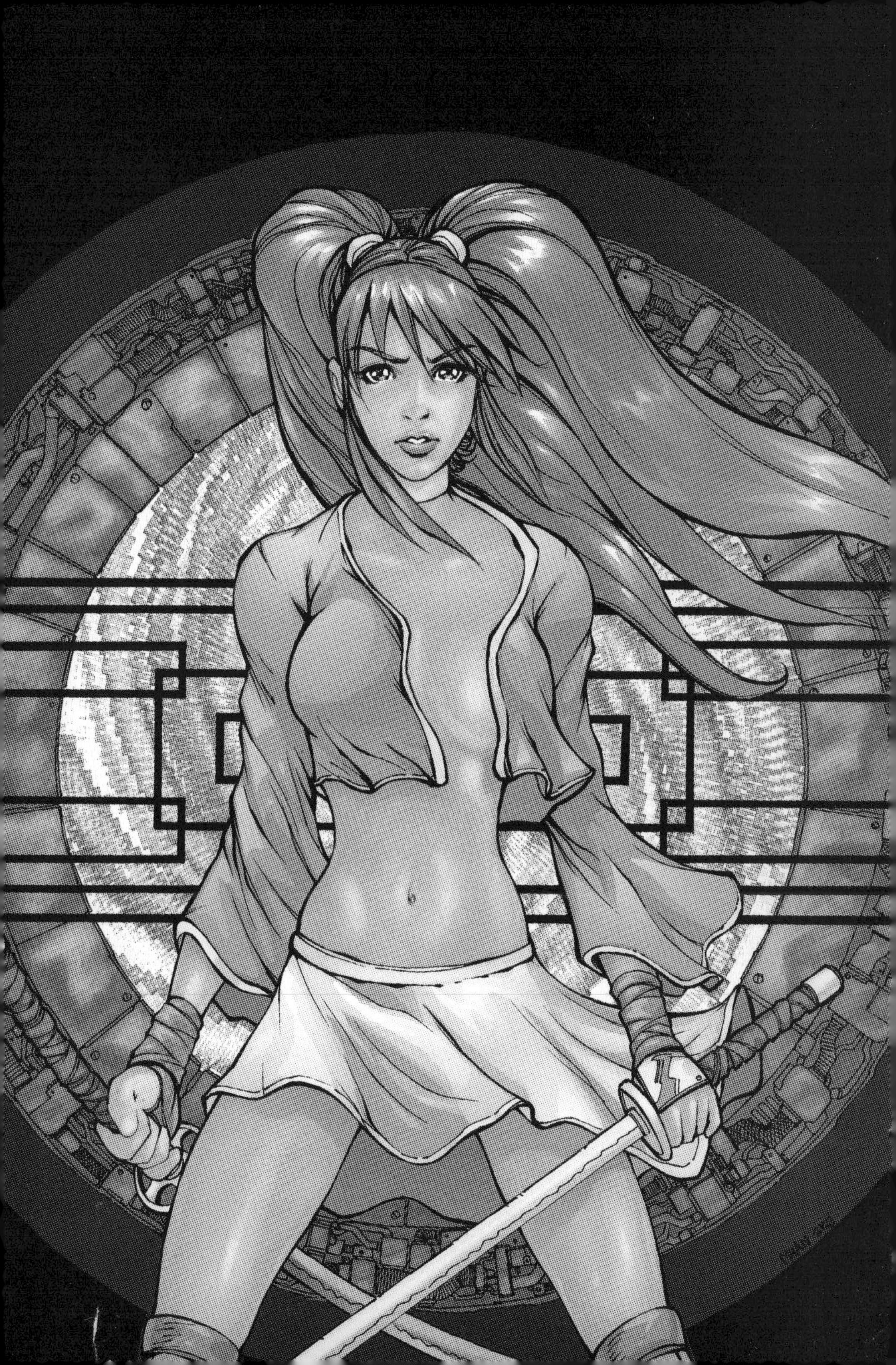

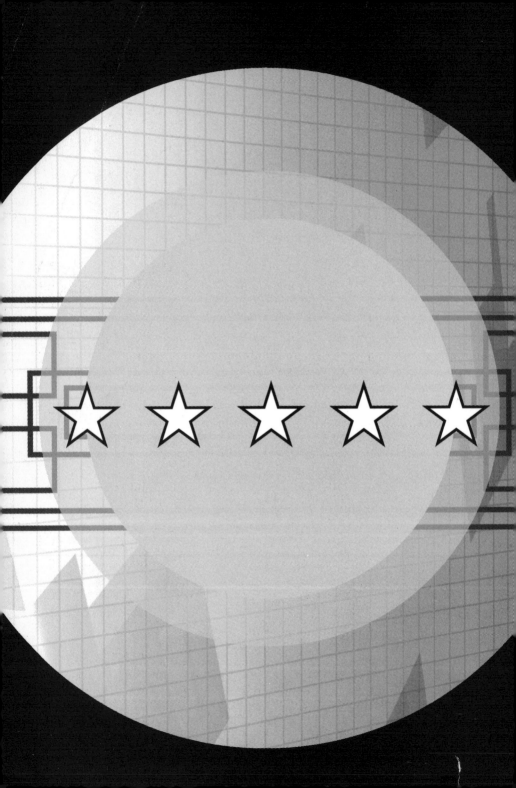

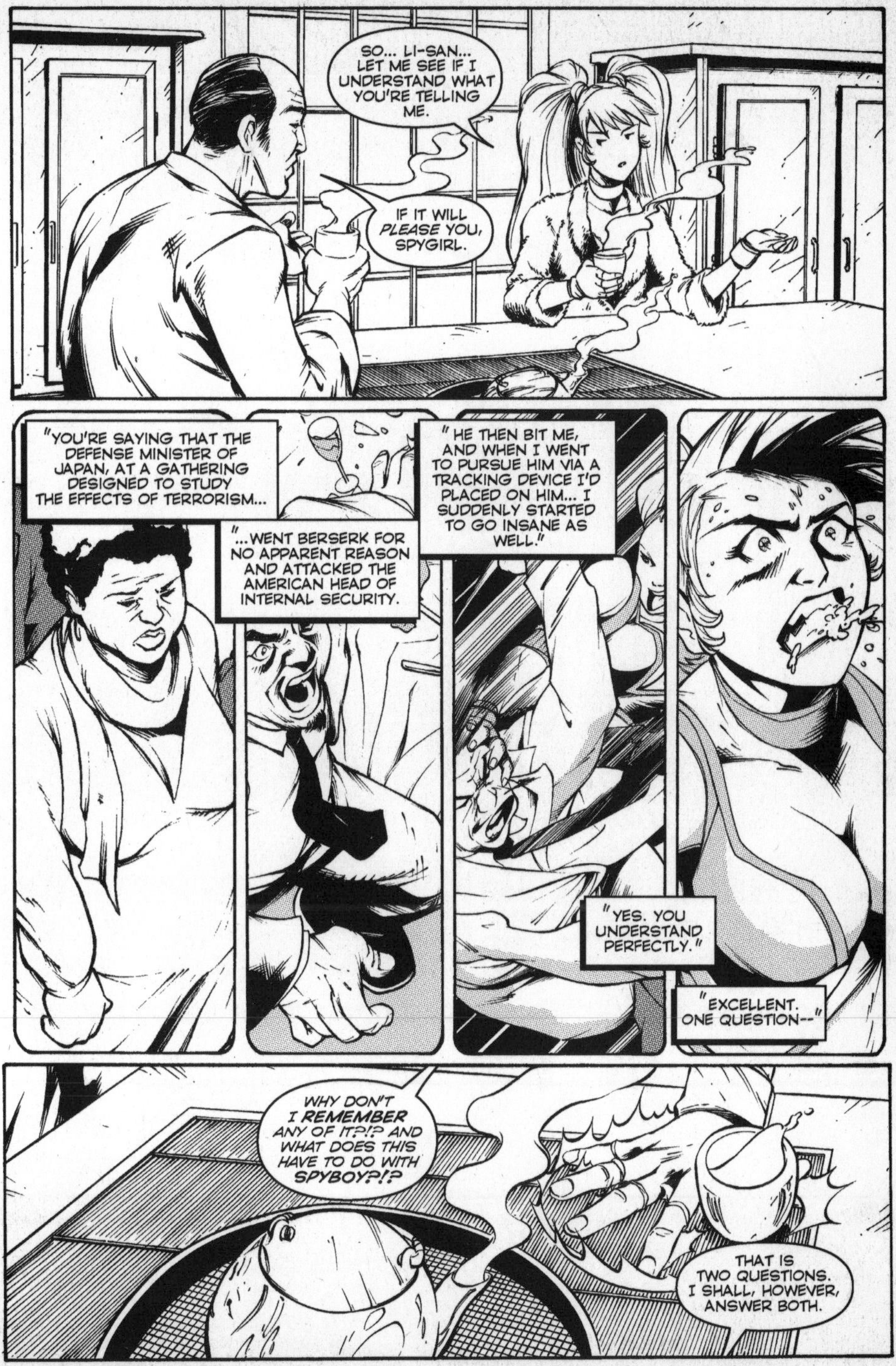
SO... LI-SAN... LET ME SEE IF I UNDERSTAND WHAT YOU'RE TELLING ME.
IF IT WILL *PLEASE* YOU, SPYGIRL.
"YOU'RE SAYING THAT THE DEFENSE MINISTER OF JAPAN, AT A GATHERING DESIGNED TO STUDY THE EFFECTS OF TERRORISM...
"...WENT BERSERK FOR NO APPARENT REASON AND ATTACKED THE AMERICAN HEAD OF INTERNAL SECURITY.
" HE THEN BIT ME, AND WHEN I WENT TO PURSUE HIM VIA A TRACKING DEVICE I'D PLACED ON HIM... I SUDDENLY STARTED TO GO INSANE AS WELL."
"YES. YOU UNDERSTAND PERFECTLY."
"EXCELLENT. ONE QUESTION--"
WHY DON'T I ***REMEMBER*** *ANY OF IT?!? AND WHAT DOES THIS HAVE TO DO WITH* ***SPYBOY?!?***
THAT IS TWO QUESTIONS. I SHALL, HOWEVER, ANSWER BOTH.

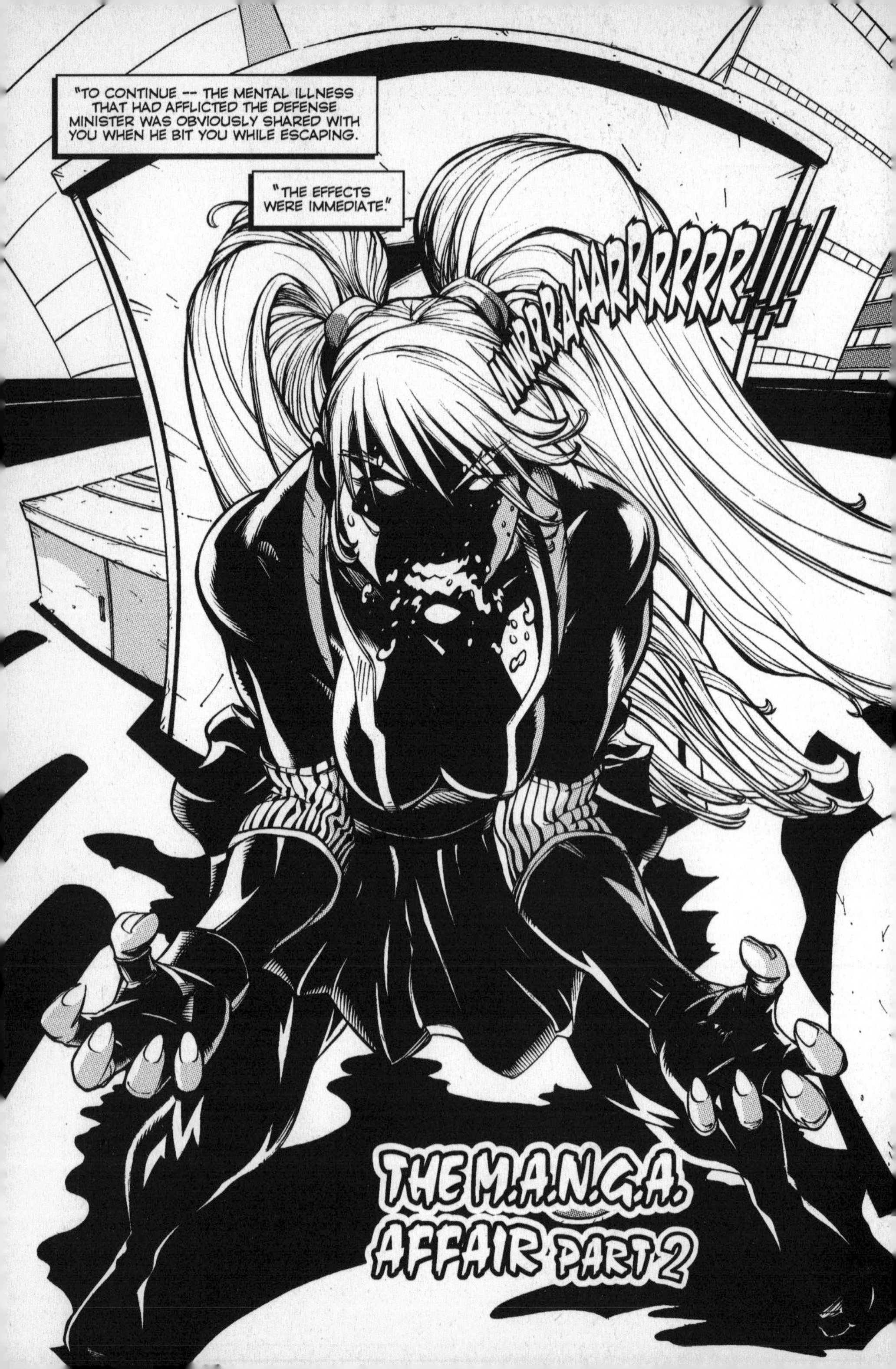
"TO CONTINUE -- THE MENTAL ILLNESS THAT HAD AFFLICTED THE DEFENSE MINISTER WAS OBVIOUSLY SHARED WITH YOU WHEN HE BIT YOU WHILE ESCAPING.
"THE EFFECTS WERE IMMEDIATE."
RRRAAARRRRRR!!!
THE M.A.N.G.A. AFFAIR PART 2

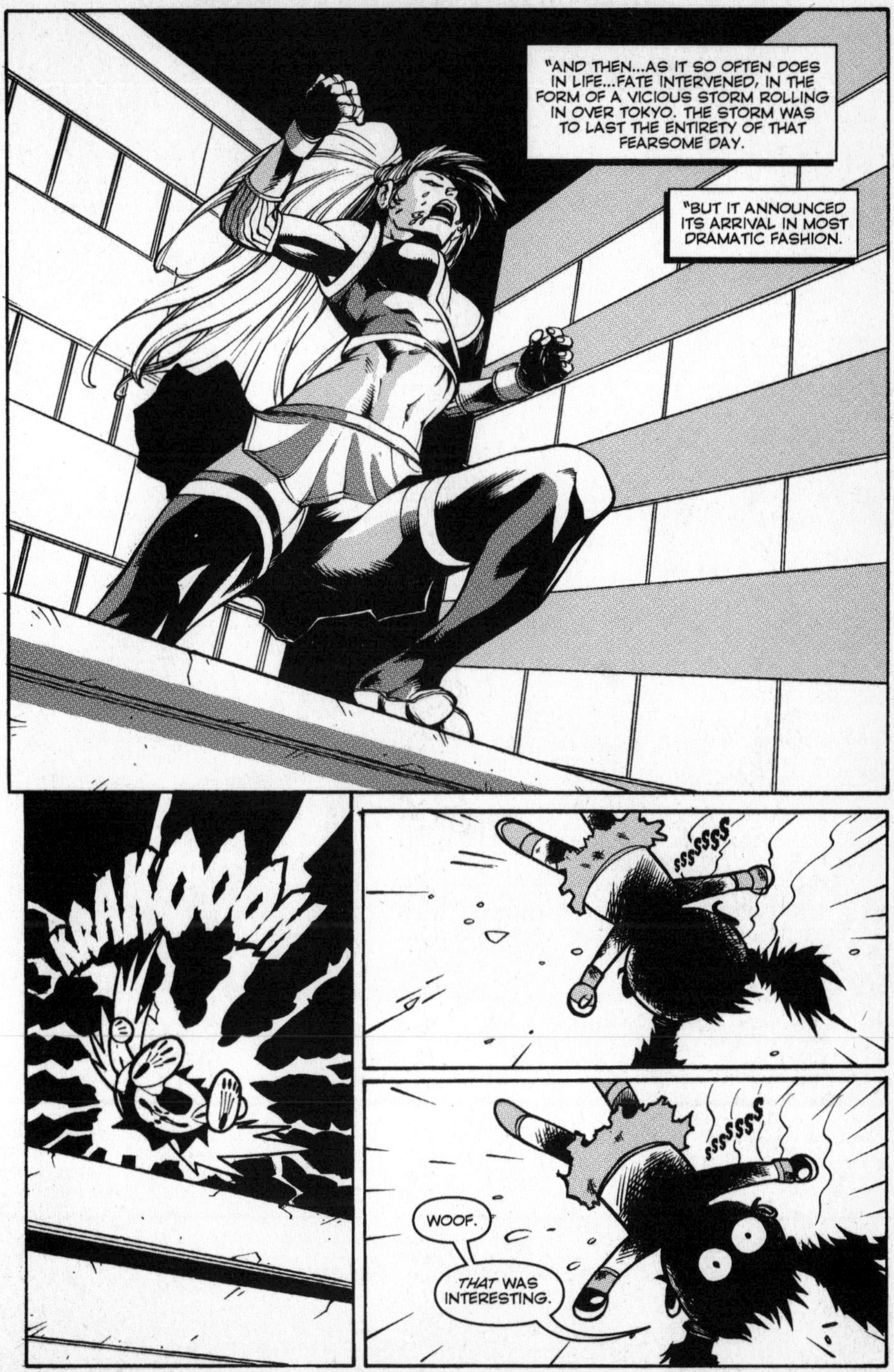
"AND THEN...AS IT SO OFTEN DOES IN LIFE...FATE INTERVENED, IN THE FORM OF A VICIOUS STORM ROLLING IN OVER TOKYO. THE STORM WAS TO LAST THE ENTIRETY OF THAT FEARSOME DAY.
"BUT IT ANNOUNCED ITS ARRIVAL IN MOST DRAMATIC FASHION.
KRAKOOOOM
SSSSSSSS
SSSSSSS
WOOF.
THAT WAS INTERESTING.

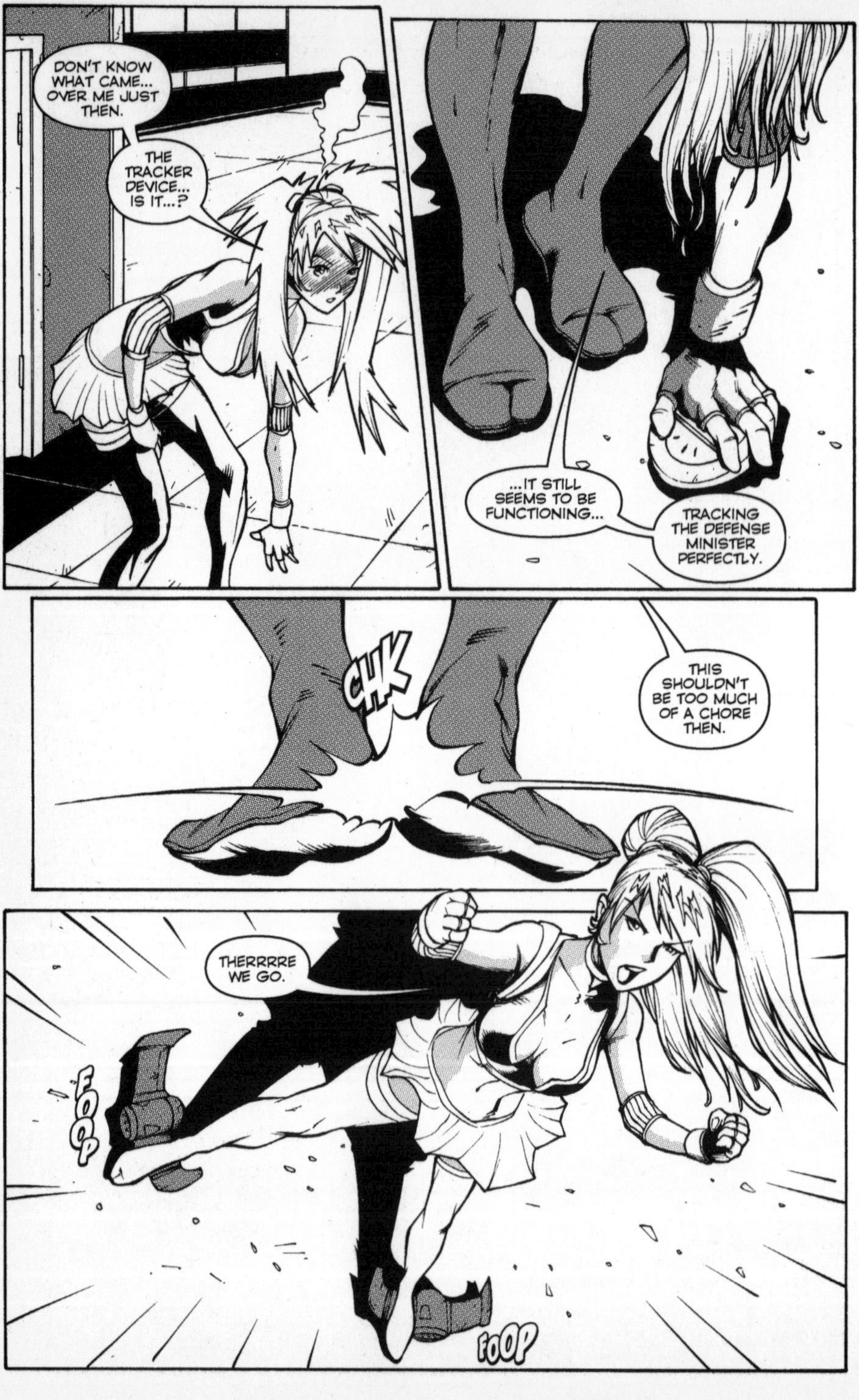
DON'T KNOW WHAT CAME... OVER ME JUST THEN.
THE TRACKER DEVICE... IS IT...?
...IT STILL SEEMS TO BE FUNCTIONING...
TRACKING THE DEFENSE MINISTER PERFECTLY.
CHK
THIS SHOULDN'T BE TOO MUCH OF A CHORE THEN.
THERRRRE WE GO.
FOOP
FOOP

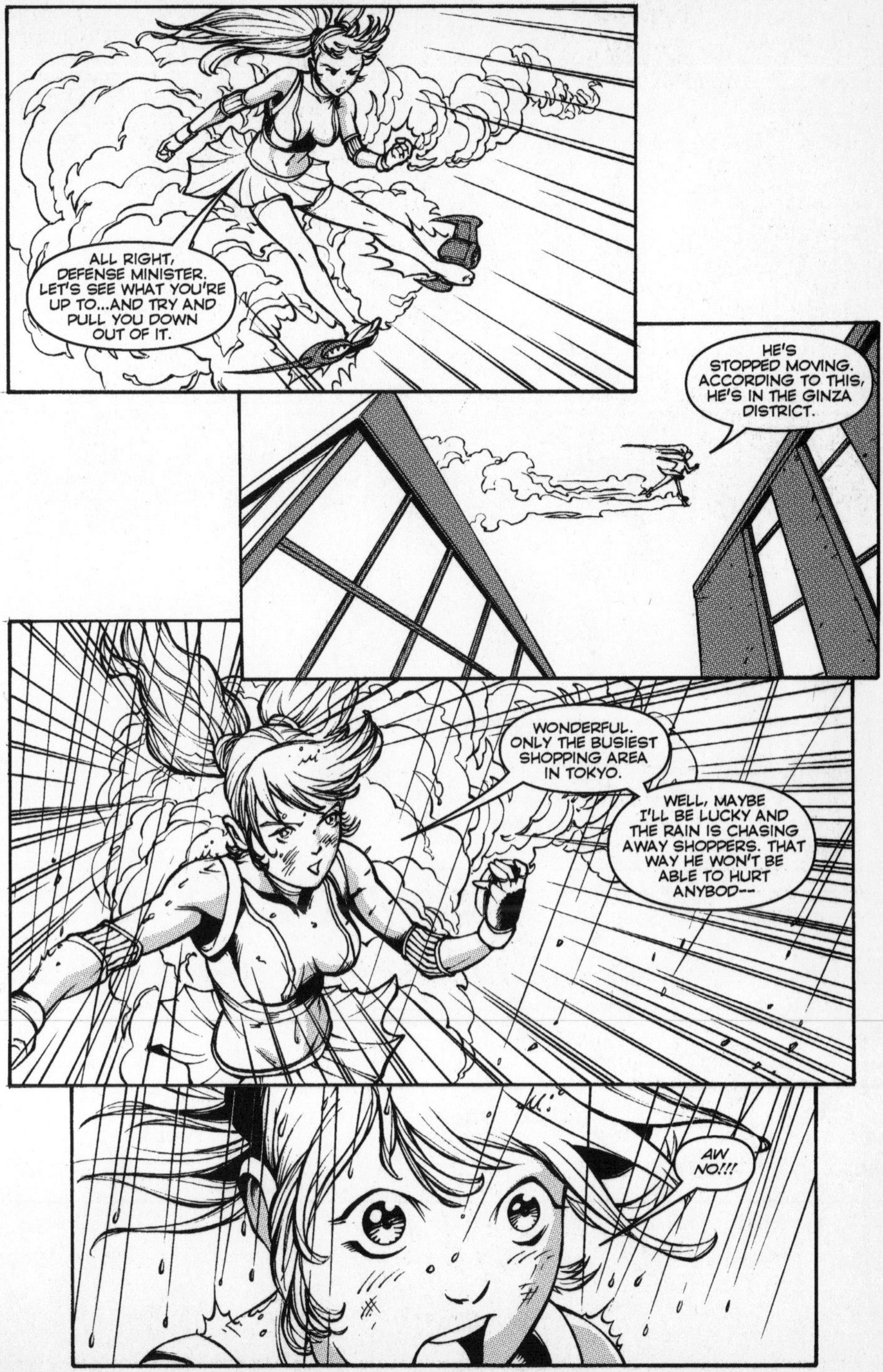
ALL RIGHT, DEFENSE MINISTER. LET'S SEE WHAT YOU'RE UP TO...AND TRY AND PULL YOU DOWN OUT OF IT.
HE'S STOPPED MOVING. ACCORDING TO THIS, HE'S IN THE GINZA DISTRICT.
WONDERFUL. ONLY THE BUSIEST SHOPPING AREA IN TOKYO.
WELL, MAYBE I'LL BE LUCKY AND THE RAIN IS CHASING AWAY SHOPPERS. THAT WAY HE WON'T BE ABLE TO HURT ANYBOD--
AW NO!!!

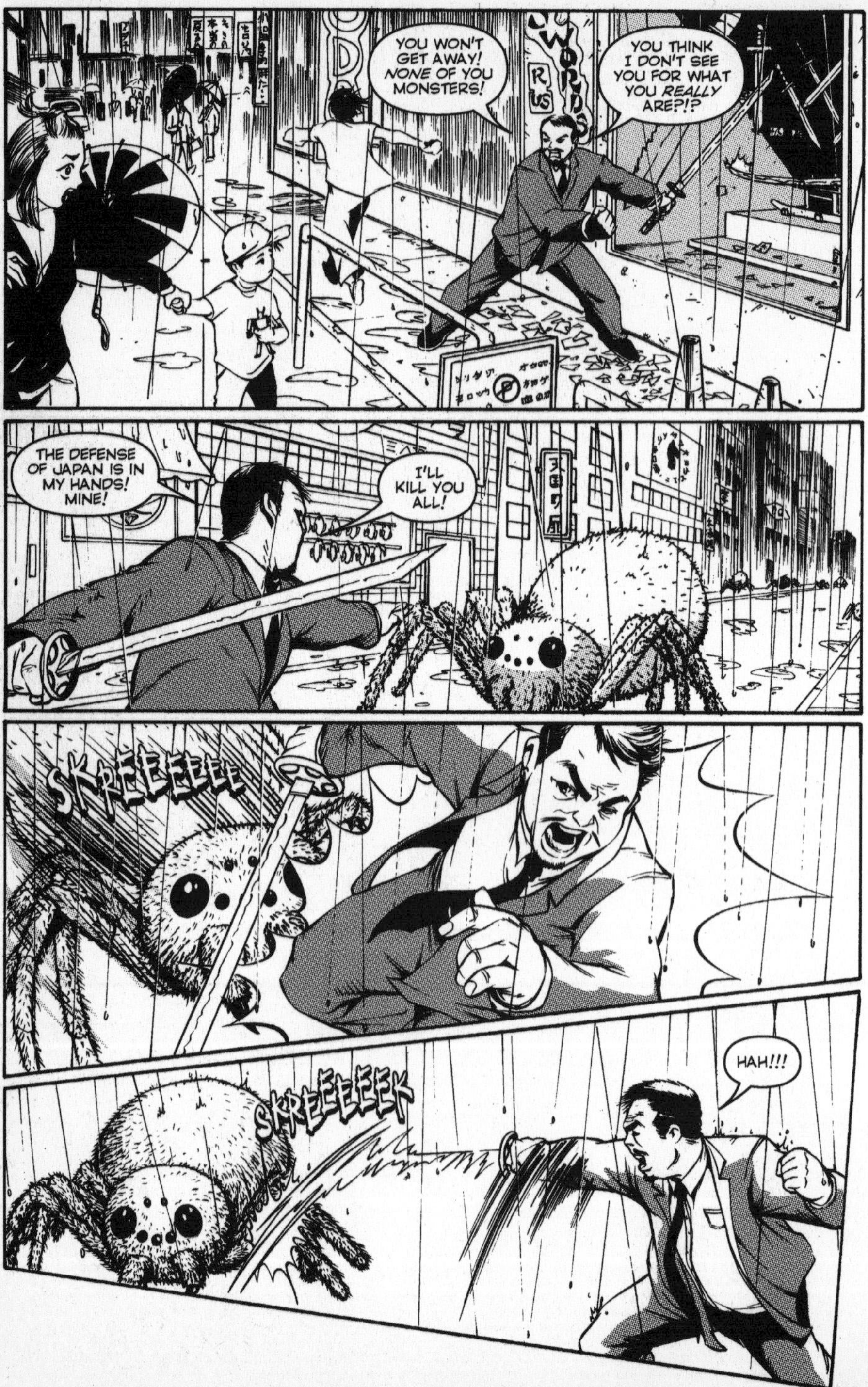
YOU WON'T GET AWAY! *NONE* OF YOU MONSTERS!
YOU THINK I DON'T SEE YOU FOR WHAT YOU *REALLY* ARE?!?
THE DEFENSE OF JAPAN IS IN MY HANDS! MINE!
I'LL KILL YOU ALL!
SKREEEEEEE
HAH!!!
SKREEEEEK

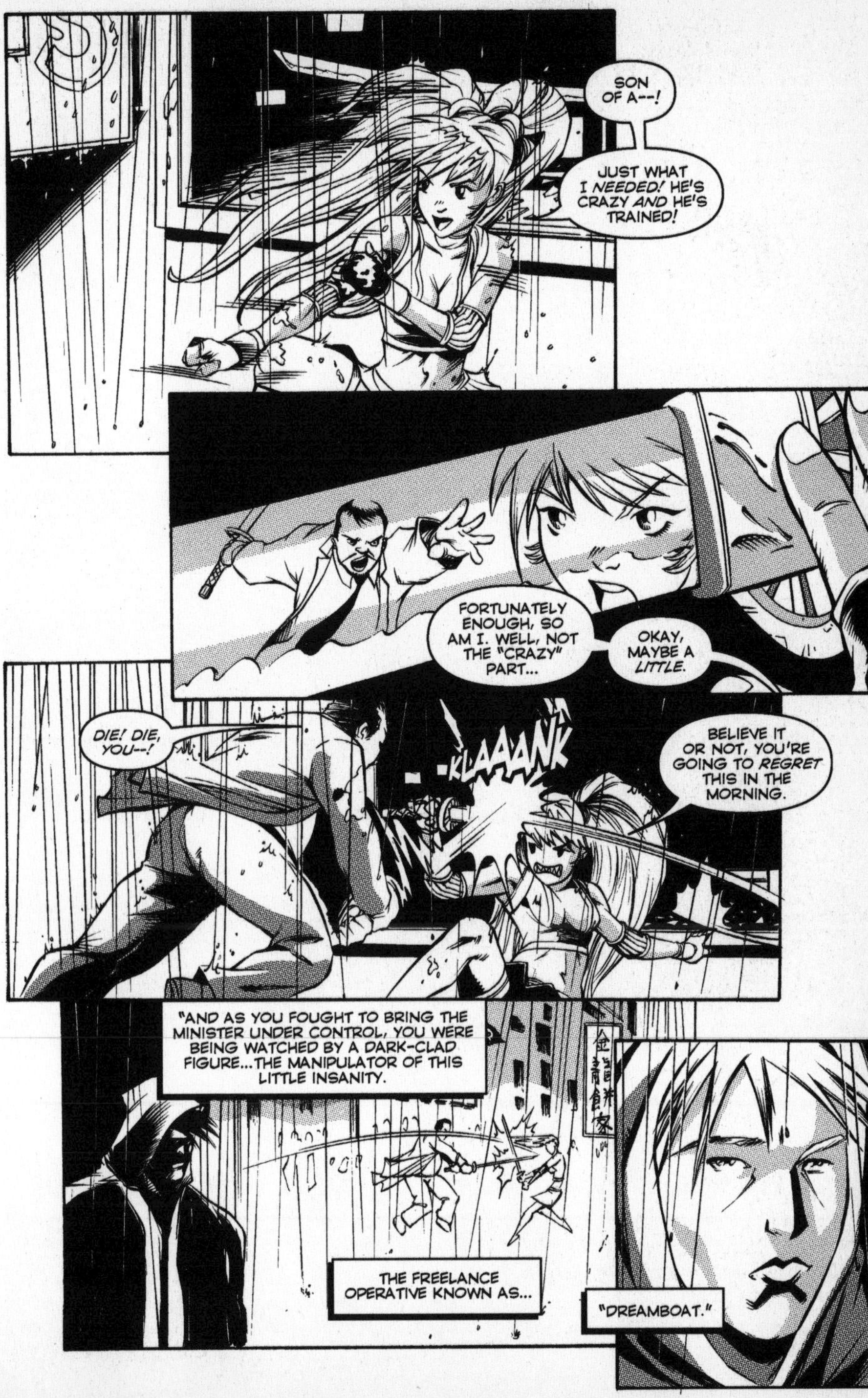
SON OF A--!
JUST WHAT I *NEEDED!* HE'S CRAZY *AND* HE'S TRAINED!
FORTUNATELY ENOUGH, SO AM I. WELL, NOT THE "CRAZY" PART...
OKAY, MAYBE A *LITTLE*.
DIE! DIE, YOU--!
KLAAANK
BELIEVE IT OR NOT, YOU'RE GOING TO *REGRET* THIS IN THE MORNING.
"AND AS YOU FOUGHT TO BRING THE MINISTER UNDER CONTROL, YOU WERE BEING WATCHED BY A DARK-CLAD FIGURE...THE MANIPULATOR OF THIS LITTLE INSANITY.
THE FREELANCE OPERATIVE KNOWN AS...
"DREAMBOAT."

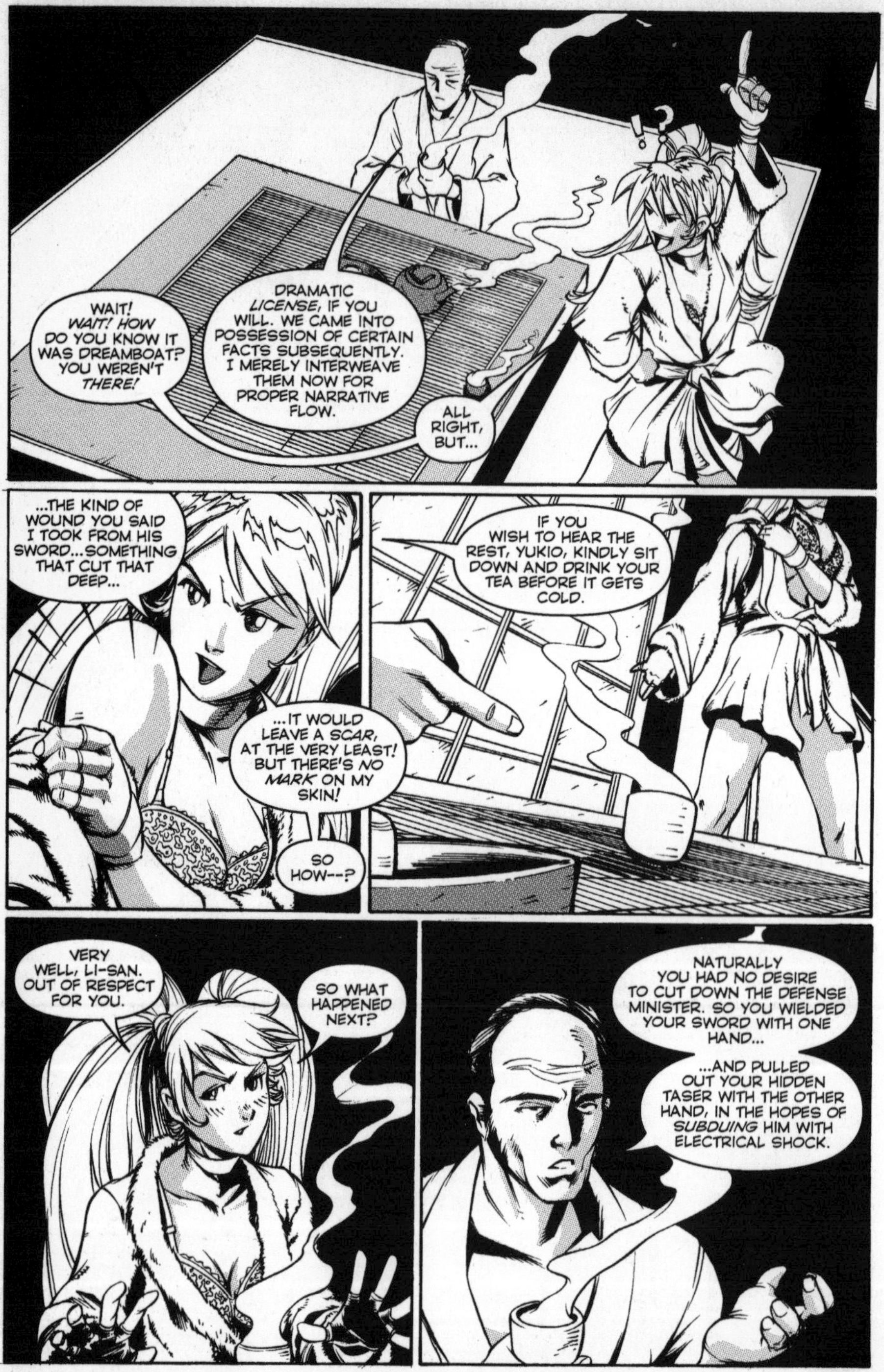

WAIT! *WAIT! HOW* DO YOU KNOW IT WAS DREAMBOAT? YOU WEREN'T *THERE!*
DRAMATIC *LICENSE,* IF YOU WILL. WE CAME INTO POSSESSION OF CERTAIN FACTS SUBSEQUENTLY. I MERELY INTERWEAVE THEM NOW FOR PROPER NARRATIVE FLOW.
ALL RIGHT, BUT...
...THE KIND OF WOUND YOU SAID I TOOK FROM HIS SWORD...SOMETHING THAT CUT THAT DEEP...
...IT WOULD LEAVE A *SCAR,* AT THE VERY LEAST! BUT THERE'S *NO MARK* ON MY SKIN!
SO HOW--?
IF YOU WISH TO HEAR THE REST, YUKIO, KINDLY SIT DOWN AND DRINK YOUR TEA BEFORE IT GETS COLD.
VERY WELL, LI-SAN. OUT OF RESPECT FOR YOU.
SO WHAT HAPPENED NEXT?
NATURALLY YOU HAD NO DESIRE TO CUT DOWN THE DEFENSE MINISTER. SO YOU WIELDED YOUR SWORD WITH ONE HAND...
...AND PULLED OUT YOUR HIDDEN TASER WITH THE OTHER HAND, IN THE HOPES OF *SUBDUING* HIM WITH ELECTRICAL SHOCK.

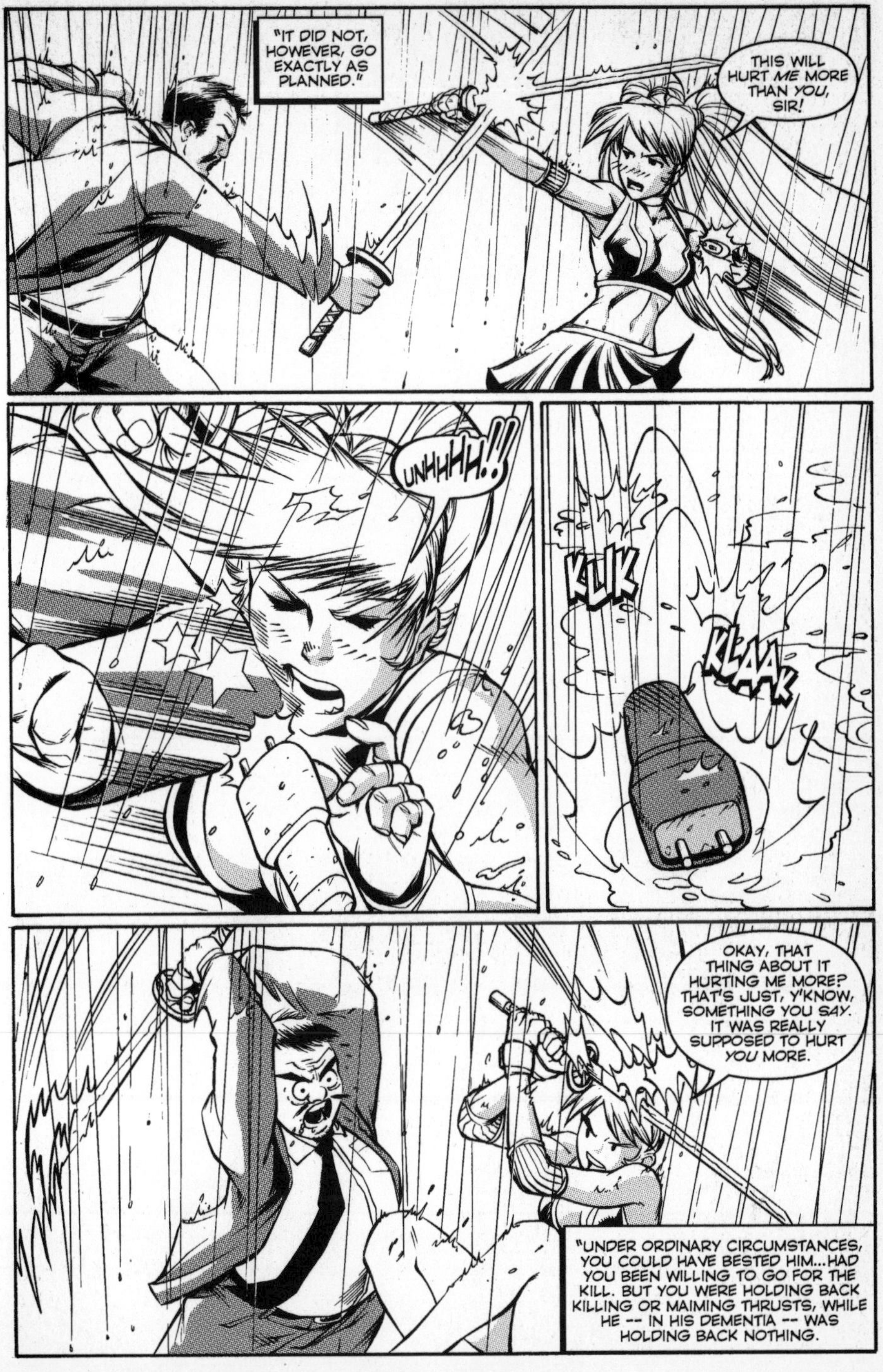
"IT DID NOT, HOWEVER, GO EXACTLY AS PLANNED."
THIS WILL HURT *ME* MORE THAN *YOU*, SIR!
UNHHHH!!!
KLIK
KLAAK
OKAY, THAT THING ABOUT IT HURTING ME MORE? THAT'S JUST, Y'KNOW, SOMETHING YOU SAY. IT WAS REALLY SUPPOSED TO HURT *YOU* MORE.
"UNDER ORDINARY CIRCUMSTANCES, YOU COULD HAVE BESTED HIM...HAD YOU BEEN WILLING TO GO FOR THE KILL. BUT YOU WERE HOLDING BACK KILLING OR MAIMING THRUSTS, WHILE HE -- IN HIS DEMENTIA -- WAS HOLDING BACK NOTHING.

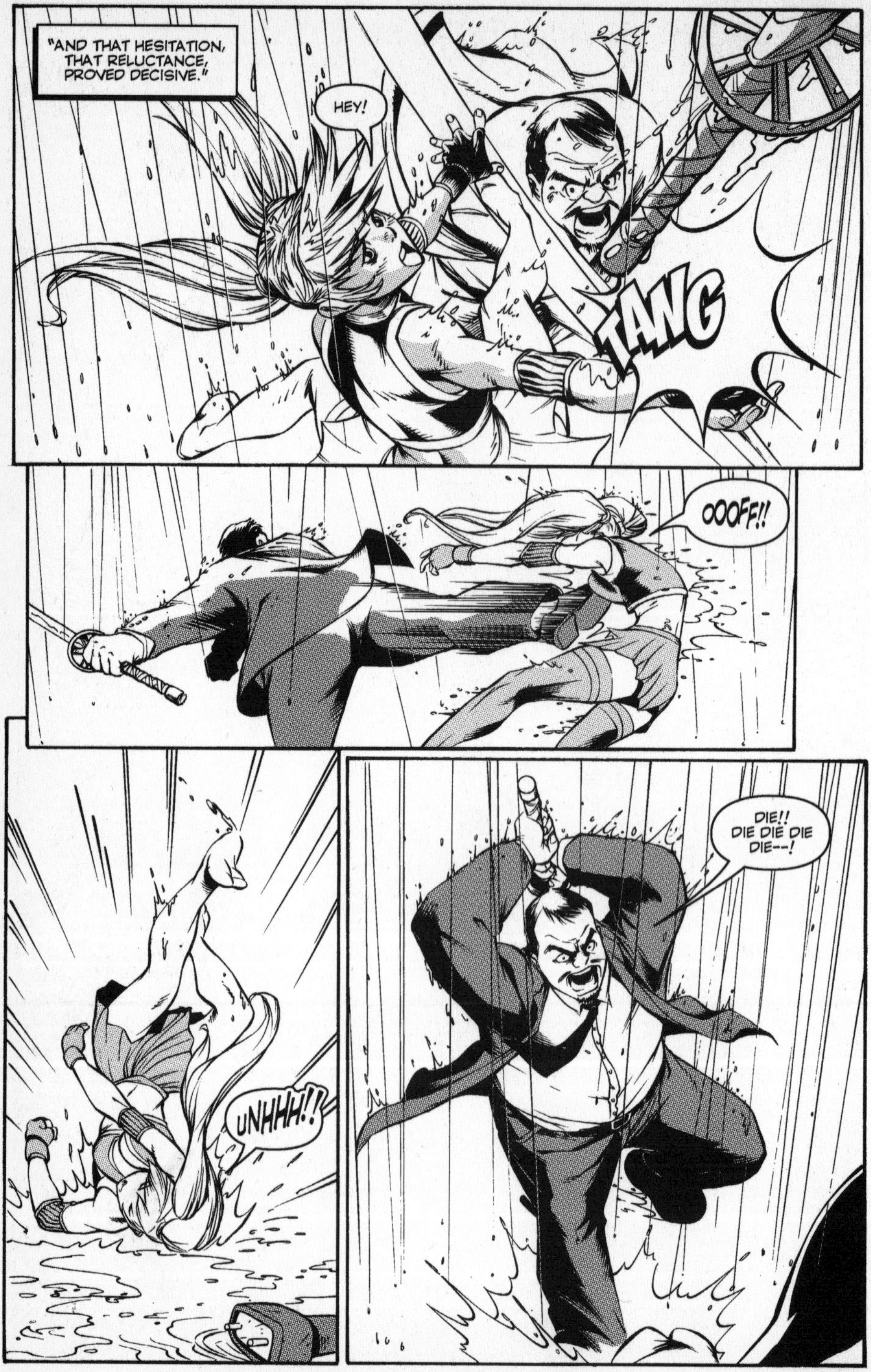
"AND THAT HESITATION, THAT RELUCTANCE, PROVED DECISIVE."
HEY!
TANG
OOOFF!!
UNHHH!!
DIE!! DIE DIE DIE DIE--!

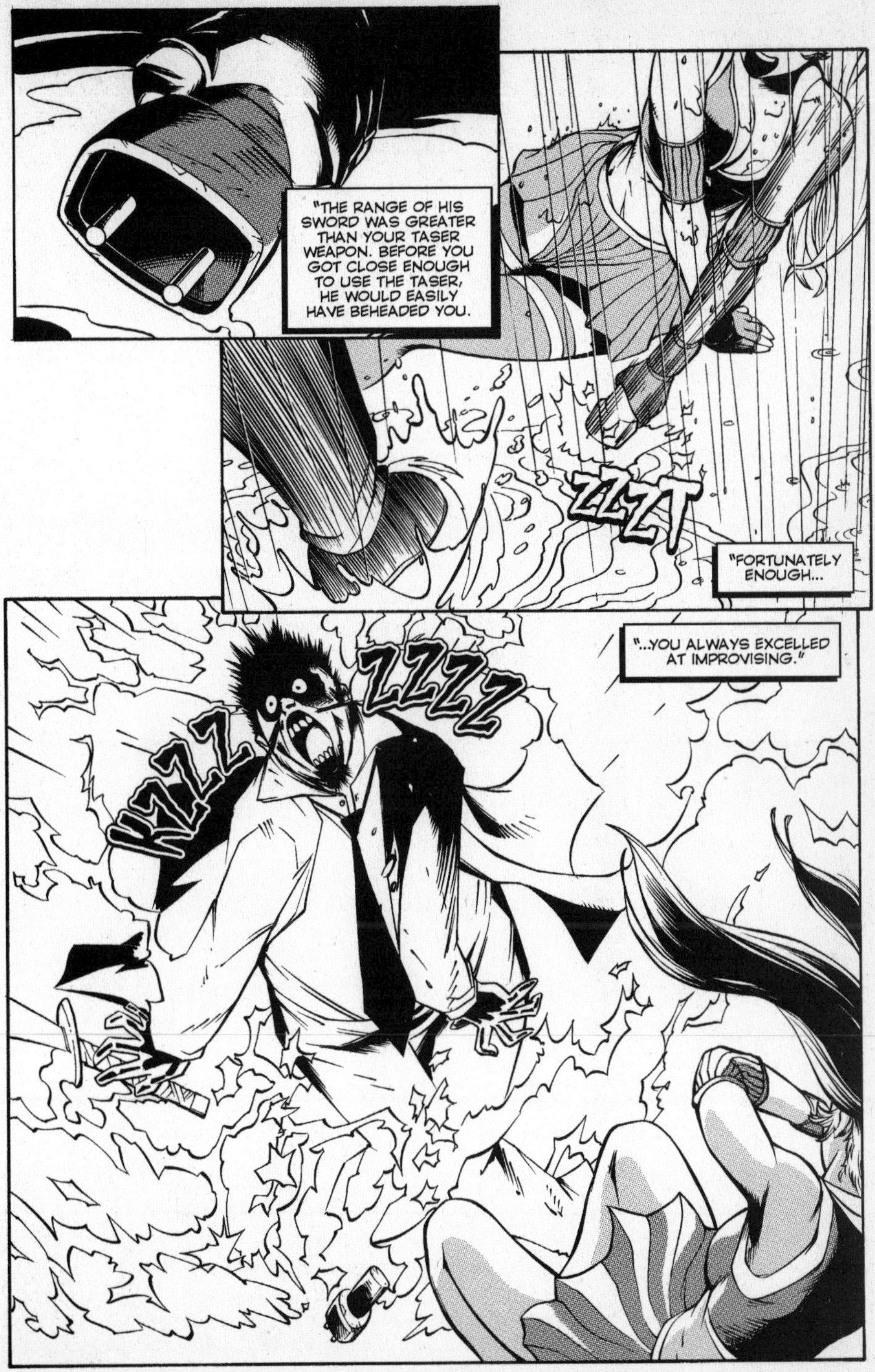
"THE RANGE OF HIS SWORD WAS GREATER THAN YOUR TASER WEAPON. BEFORE YOU GOT CLOSE ENOUGH TO USE THE TASER, HE WOULD EASILY HAVE BEHEADED YOU.
ZZZT
"FORTUNATELY ENOUGH...
"...YOU ALWAYS EXCELLED AT IMPROVISING."
ZZZZ
KZZZ

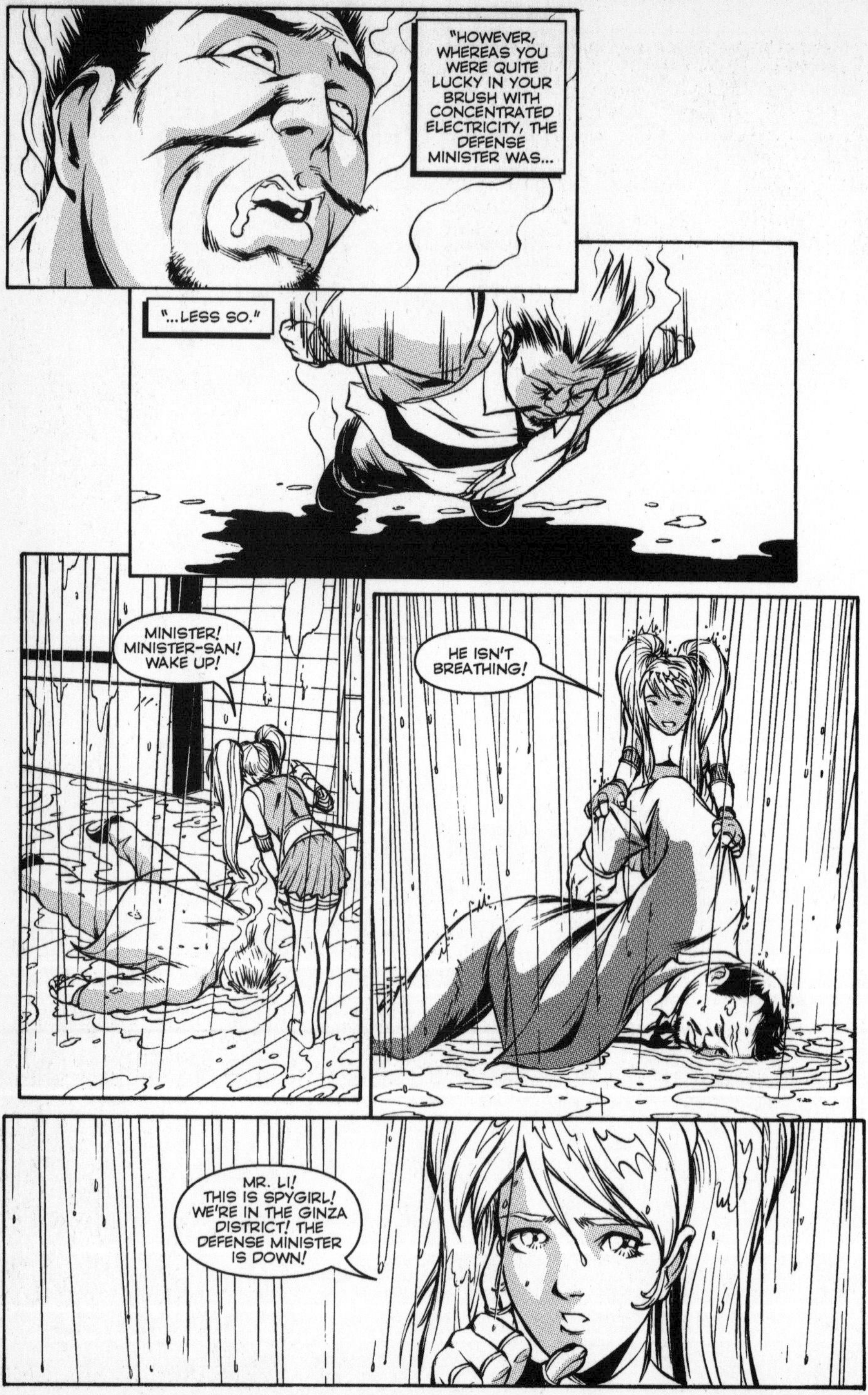
"HOWEVER, WHEREAS YOU WERE QUITE LUCKY IN YOUR BRUSH WITH CONCENTRATED ELECTRICITY, THE DEFENSE MINISTER WAS...
"...LESS SO."
MINISTER! MINISTER-SAN! WAKE UP!
HE ISN'T BREATHING!
MR. LI! THIS IS SPYGIRL! WE'RE IN THE GINZA DISTRICT! THE DEFENSE MINISTER IS DOWN!

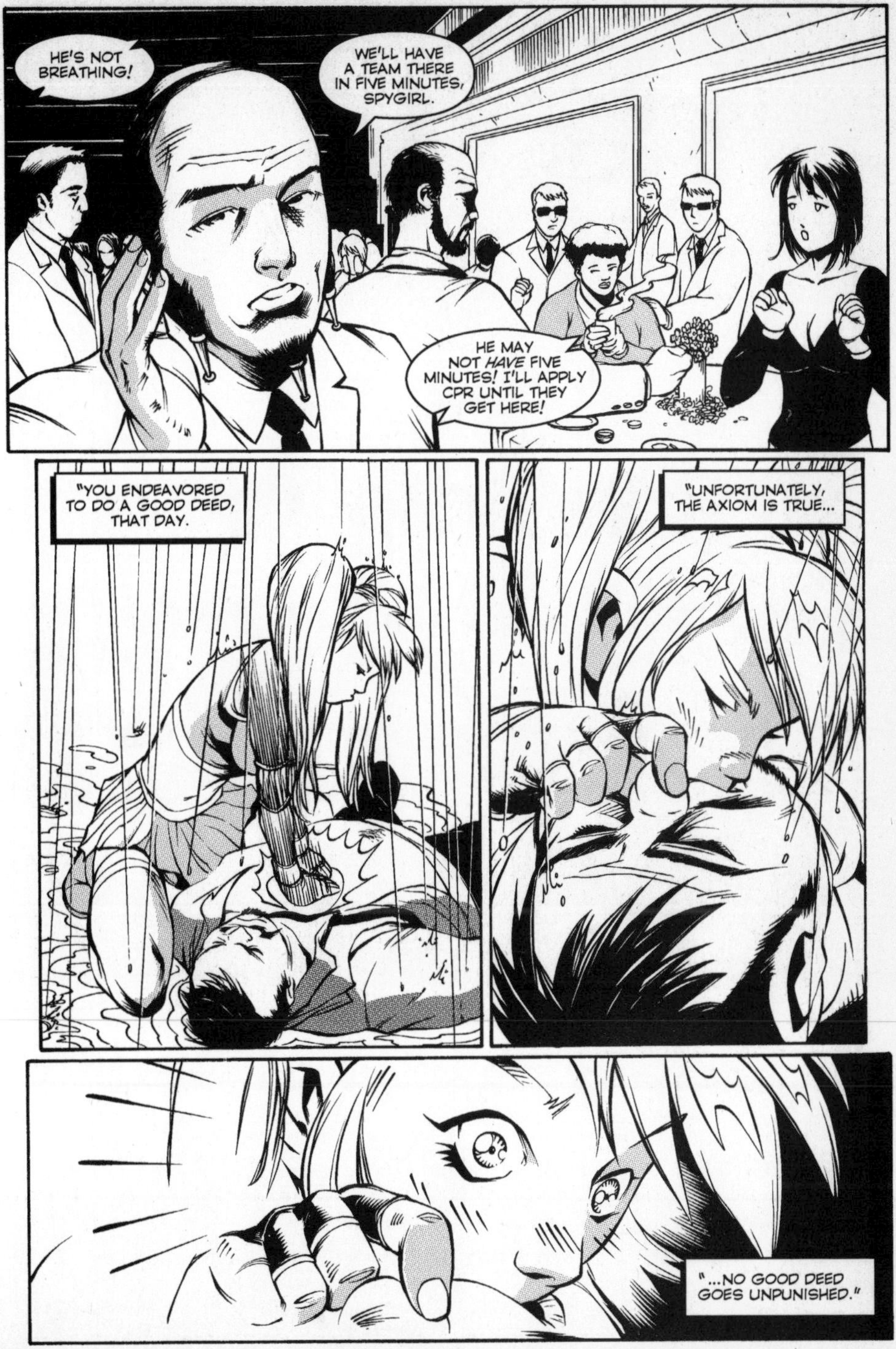

HE'S NOT BREATHING!
WE'LL HAVE A TEAM THERE IN FIVE MINUTES, SPYGIRL.
HE MAY NOT *HAVE* FIVE MINUTES! I'LL APPLY CPR UNTIL THEY GET HERE!
"YOU ENDEAVORED TO DO A GOOD DEED, THAT DAY.
"UNFORTUNATELY, THE AXIOM IS TRUE...
"...NO GOOD DEED GOES UNPUNISHED."

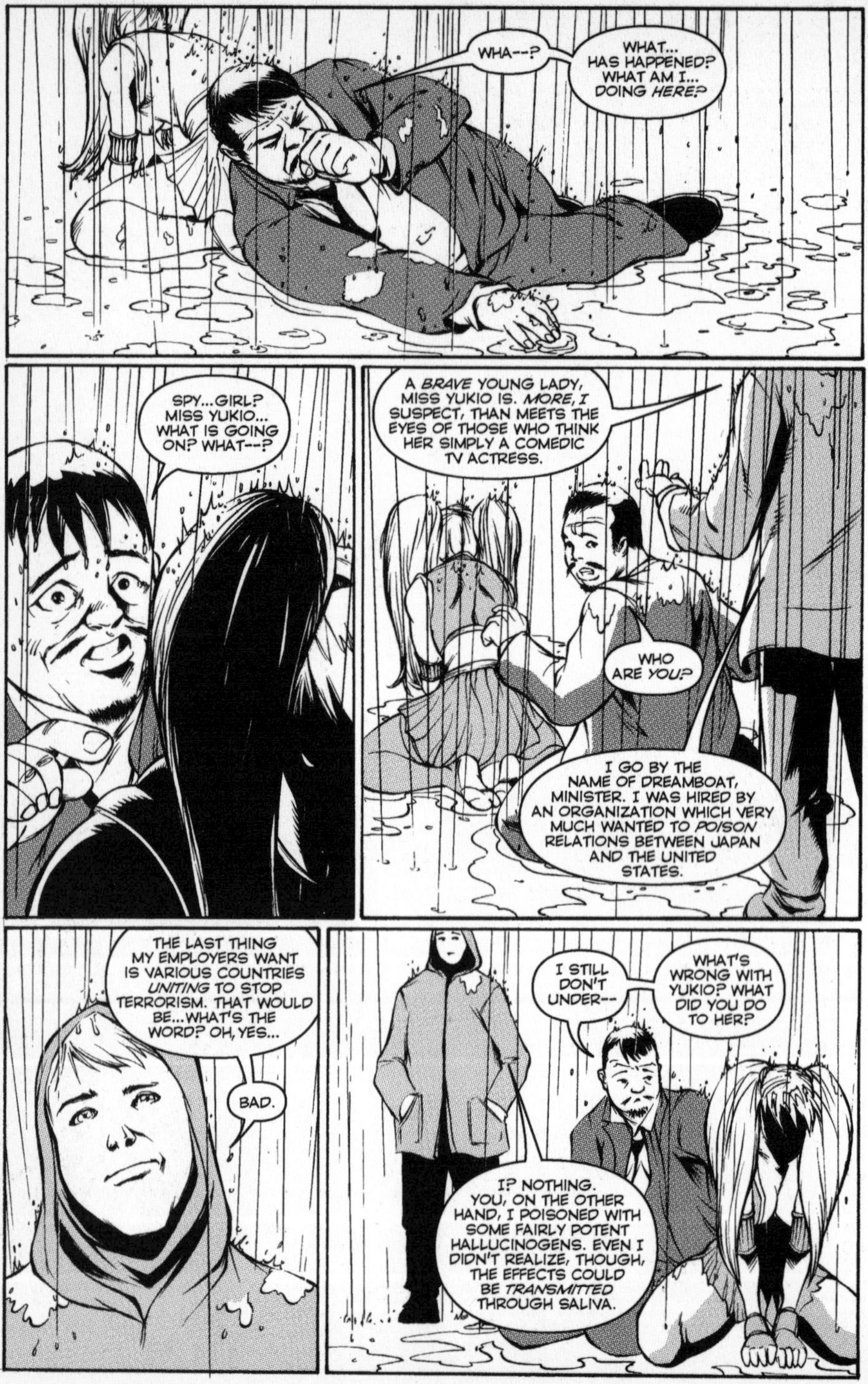
WHA--?
WHAT... HAS HAPPENED? WHAT AM I... DOING *HERE*?
SPY...GIRL? MISS YUKIO... WHAT IS GOING ON? WHAT--?
A *BRAVE* YOUNG LADY, MISS YUKIO IS. *MORE, I* SUSPECT, THAN MEETS THE EYES OF THOSE WHO THINK HER SIMPLY A COMEDIC TV ACTRESS.
WHO ARE *YOU*?
I GO BY THE NAME OF DREAMBOAT, MINISTER. I WAS HIRED BY AN ORGANIZATION WHICH VERY MUCH WANTED TO *POISON* RELATIONS BETWEEN JAPAN AND THE UNITED STATES.
THE LAST THING MY EMPLOYERS WANT IS VARIOUS COUNTRIES *UNITING* TO STOP TERRORISM. THAT WOULD BE...WHAT'S THE WORD? OH, YES...
BAD.
I STILL DON'T UNDER--
WHAT'S WRONG WITH YUKIO? WHAT DID YOU DO TO HER?
I? NOTHING. YOU, ON THE OTHER HAND, I POISONED WITH SOME FAIRLY POTENT HALLUCINOGENS. EVEN I DIDN'T REALIZE, THOUGH, THE EFFECTS COULD BE *TRANSMITTED* THROUGH SALIVA.

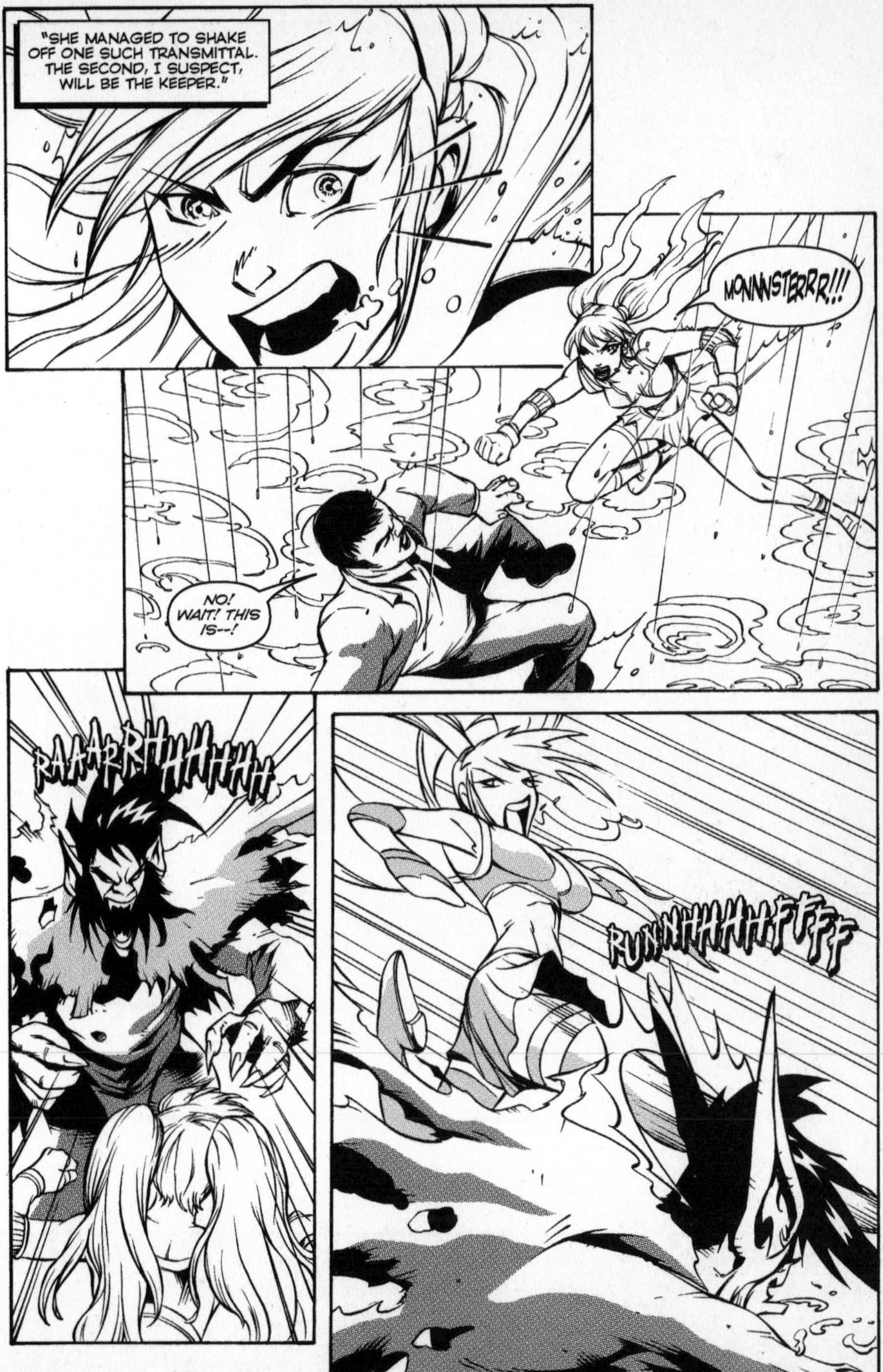
"SHE MANAGED TO SHAKE OFF ONE SUCH TRANSMITTAL. THE SECOND, I SUSPECT, WILL BE THE KEEPER."
MONNNSTERRR!!!
NO! WAIT! THIS IS--!
RAAARRHHHHHH
RUNNHHAHHFFFF

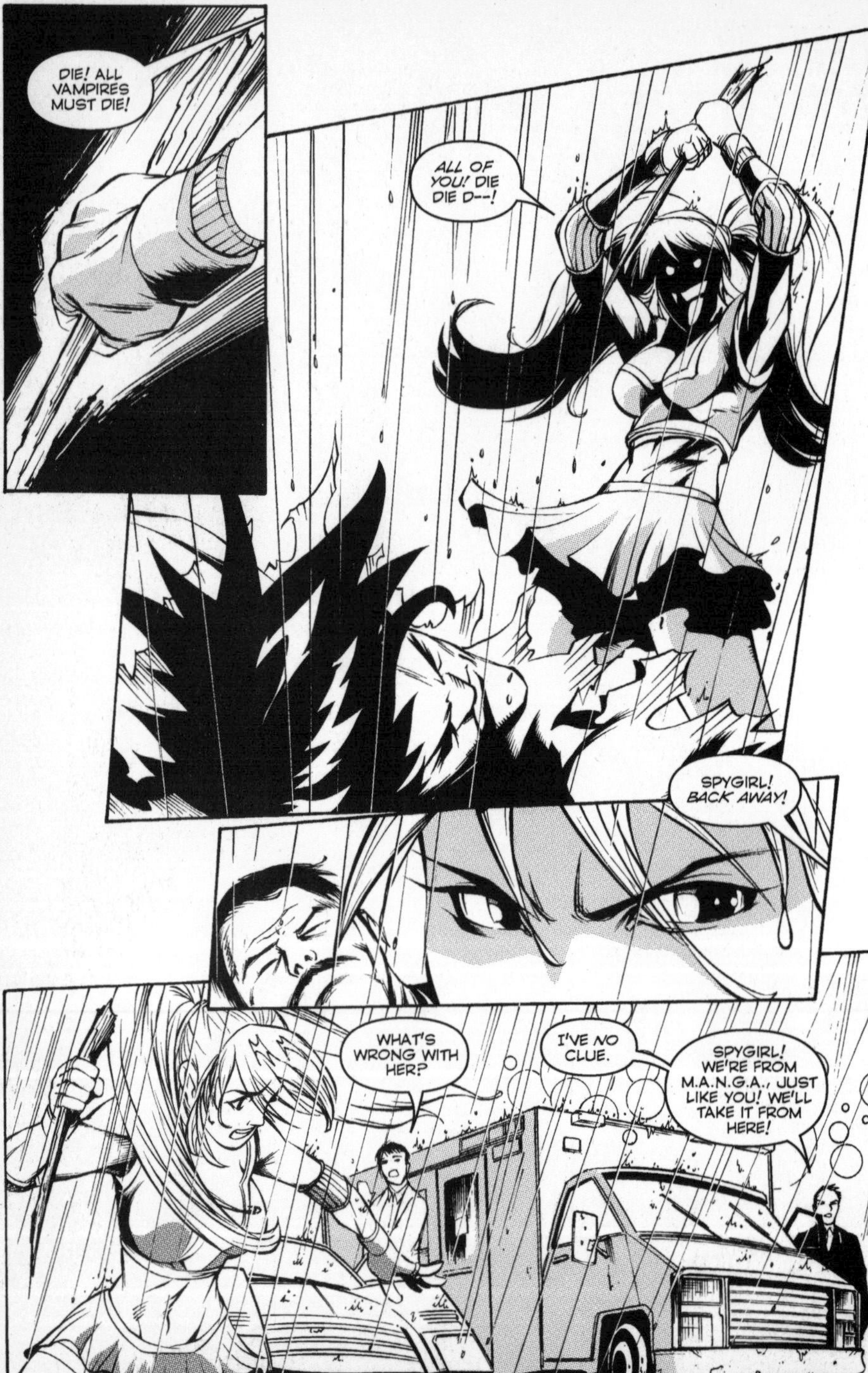
DIE! ALL VAMPIRES MUST DIE!
ALL OF YOU! DIE DIE D--!
SPYGIRL! BACK AWAY!
WHAT'S WRONG WITH HER?
I'VE NO CLUE.
SPYGIRL! WE'RE FROM M.A.N.G.A., JUST LIKE YOU! WE'LL TAKE IT FROM HERE!

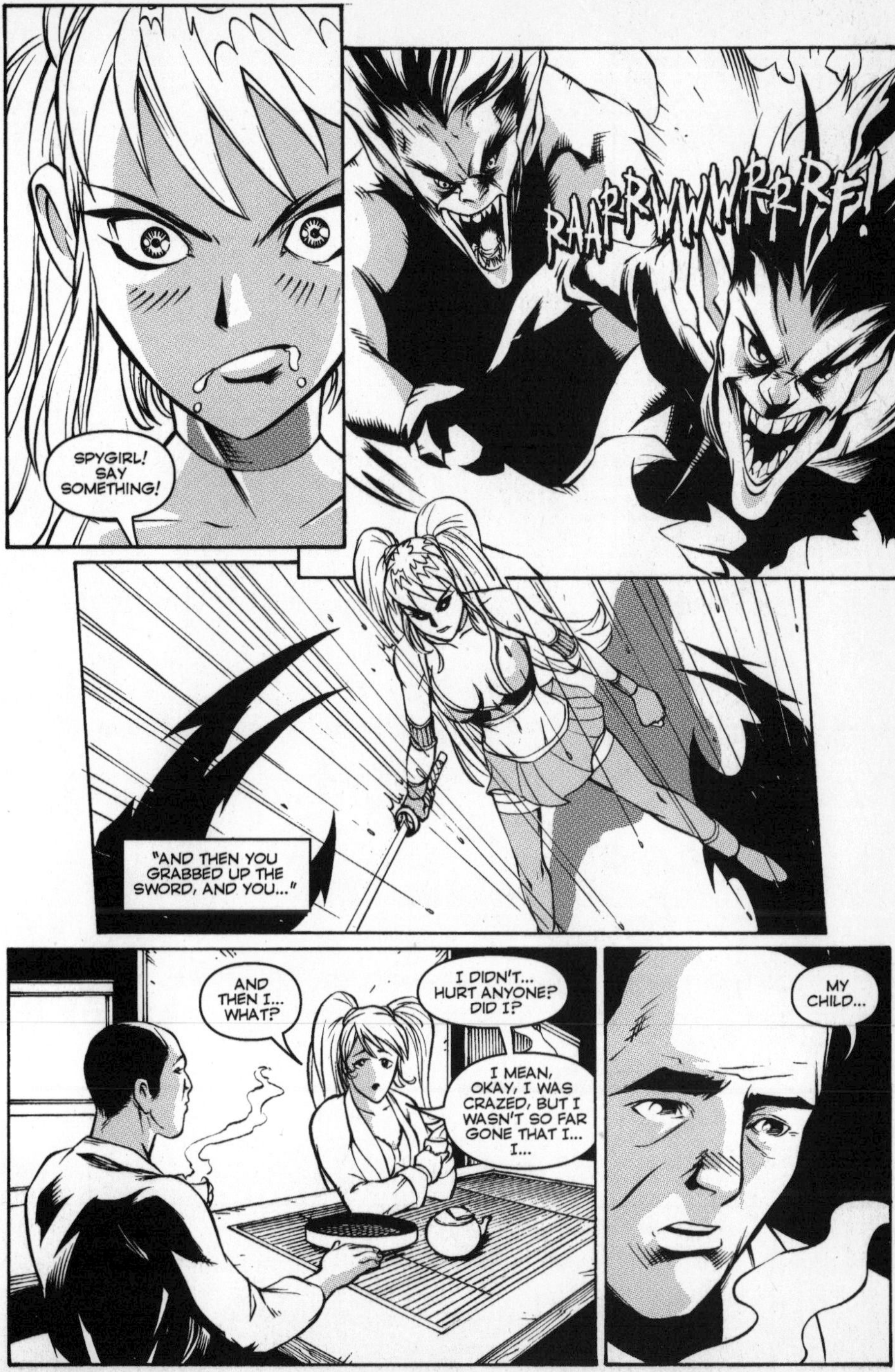
SPYGIRL! SAY SOMETHING!
RAARRWWWRRRRF!
"AND THEN YOU GRABBED UP THE SWORD, AND YOU..."
AND THEN I... WHAT?
I DIDN'T... HURT ANYONE? DID I?
I MEAN, OKAY, I WAS CRAZED, BUT I WASN'T SO FAR GONE THAT I... I...
MY CHILD...

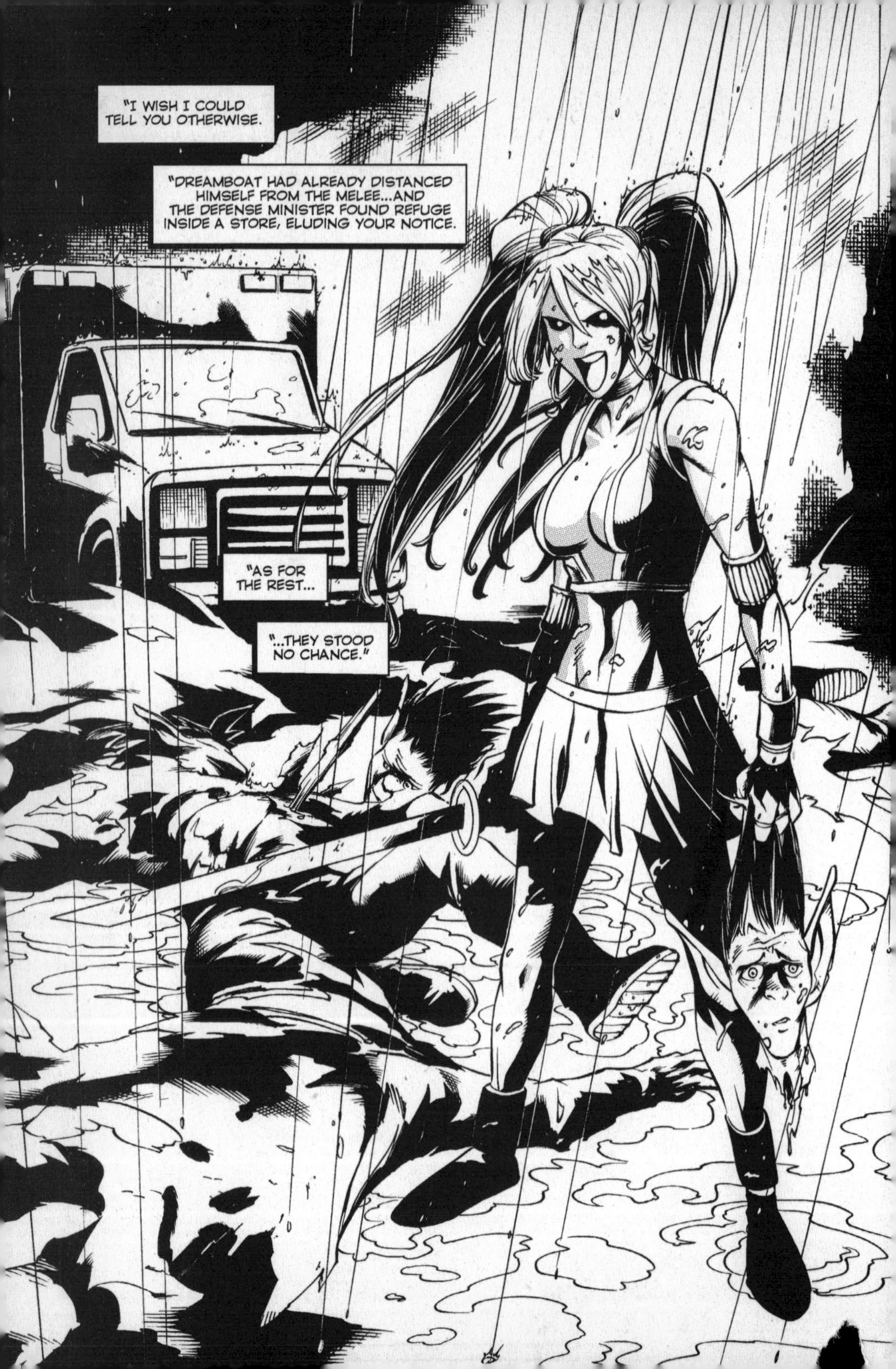
"I WISH I COULD TELL YOU OTHERWISE.
"DREAMBOAT HAD ALREADY DISTANCED HIMSELF FROM THE MELEE...AND THE DEFENSE MINISTER FOUND REFUGE INSIDE A STORE, ELUDING YOUR NOTICE.
"AS FOR THE REST...
"...THEY STOOD NO CHANCE."

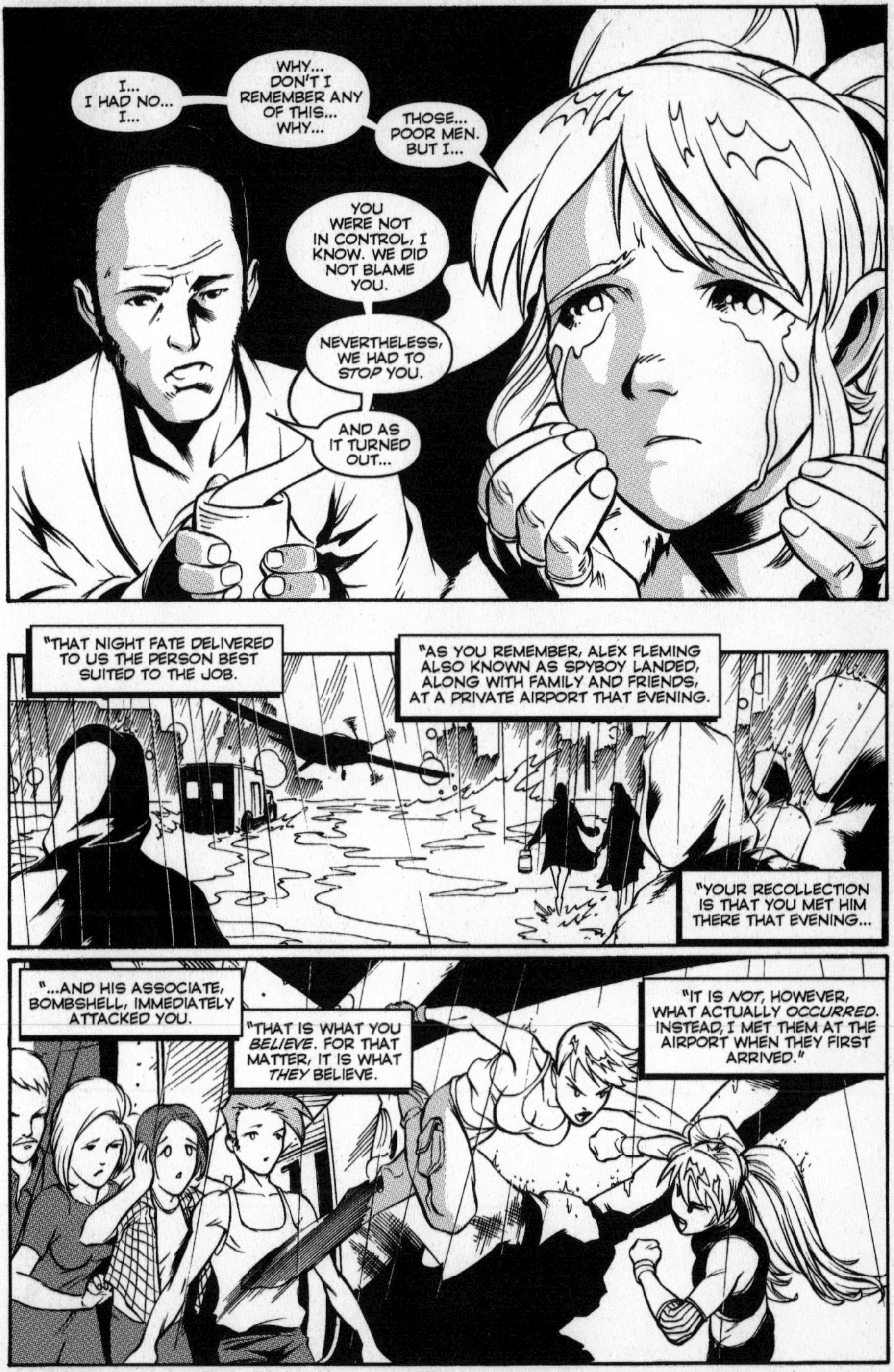
I... I HAD NO... I...
WHY... DON'T I REMEMBER ANY OF THIS... WHY...
THOSE... POOR MEN. BUT I...
YOU WERE NOT IN CONTROL, I KNOW. WE DID NOT BLAME YOU.
NEVERTHELESS, WE HAD TO *STOP* YOU.
AND AS IT TURNED OUT...
"THAT NIGHT FATE DELIVERED TO US THE PERSON BEST SUITED TO THE JOB.
"AS YOU REMEMBER, ALEX FLEMING ALSO KNOWN AS SPYBOY LANDED, ALONG WITH FAMILY AND FRIENDS, AT A PRIVATE AIRPORT THAT EVENING.
"YOUR RECOLLECTION IS THAT YOU MET HIM THERE THAT EVENING...
"...AND HIS ASSOCIATE, BOMBSHELL, IMMEDIATELY ATTACKED YOU.
"THAT IS WHAT YOU *BELIEVE*. FOR THAT MATTER, IT IS WHAT *THEY* BELIEVE.
"IT IS *NOT*, HOWEVER, WHAT ACTUALLY *OCCURRED*. INSTEAD, I MET THEM AT THE AIRPORT WHEN THEY FIRST ARRIVED."

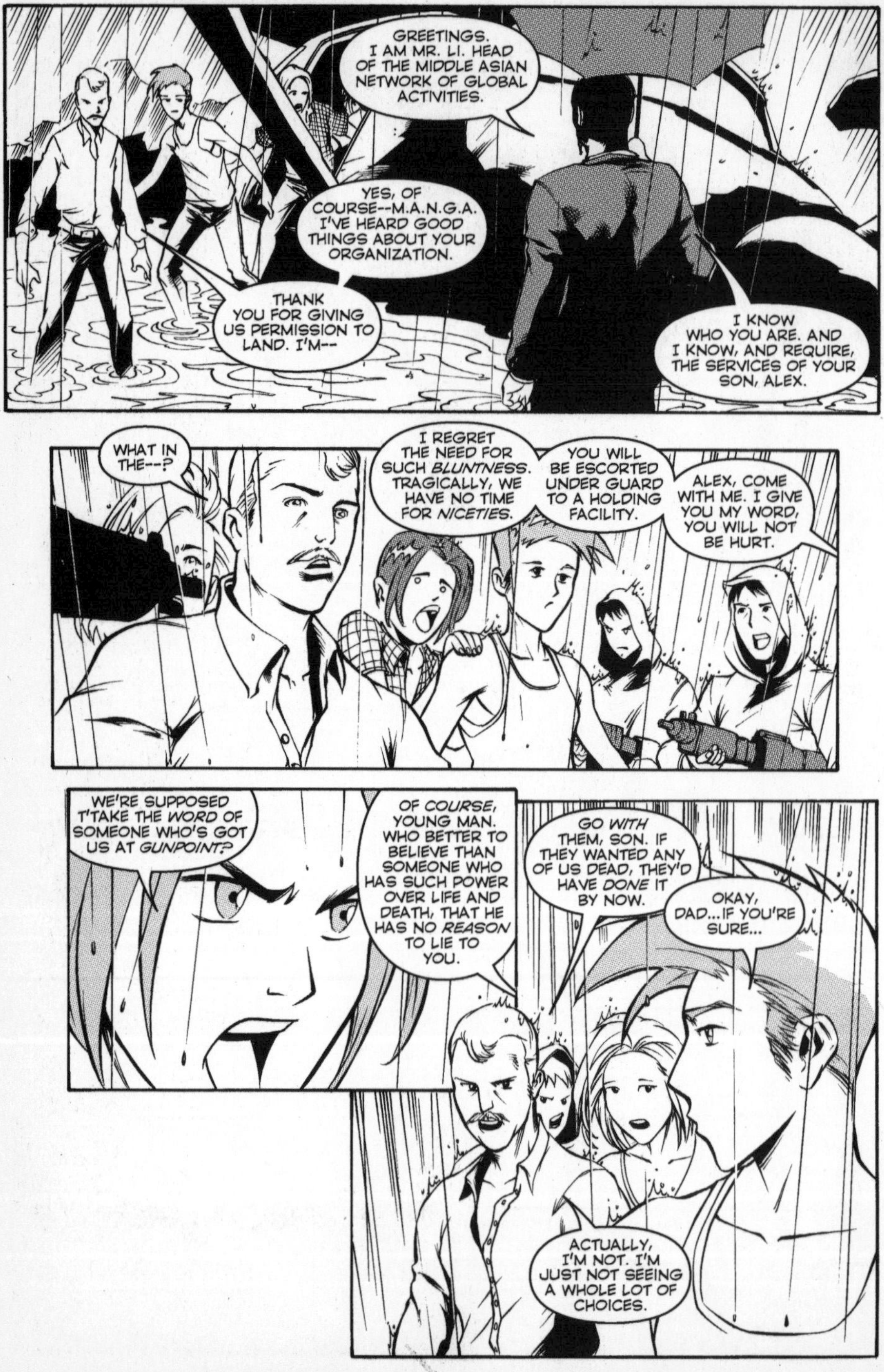
GREETINGS. I AM MR. LI. HEAD OF THE MIDDLE ASIAN NETWORK OF GLOBAL ACTIVITIES.
YES, OF COURSE--M.A.N.G.A. I'VE HEARD GOOD THINGS ABOUT YOUR ORGANIZATION.
THANK YOU FOR GIVING US PERMISSION TO LAND. I'M--
I KNOW WHO YOU ARE. AND I KNOW, AND REQUIRE, THE SERVICES OF YOUR SON, ALEX.
WHAT IN THE--?
I REGRET THE NEED FOR SUCH *BLUNTNESS*. TRAGICALLY, WE HAVE NO TIME FOR *NICETIES*.
YOU WILL BE ESCORTED UNDER GUARD TO A HOLDING FACILITY.
ALEX, COME WITH ME. I GIVE YOU MY WORD, YOU WILL NOT BE HURT.
WE'RE SUPPOSED T'TAKE THE *WORD* OF SOMEONE WHO'S GOT US AT *GUNPOINT?*
OF COURSE, YOUNG MAN. WHO BETTER TO BELIEVE THAN SOMEONE WHO HAS SUCH POWER OVER LIFE AND DEATH, THAT HE HAS NO *REASON* TO LIE TO YOU.
GO *WITH* THEM, SON. IF THEY WANTED ANY OF US DEAD, THEY'D HAVE *DONE* IT BY NOW.
OKAY, DAD...IF YOU'RE SURE...
ACTUALLY, I'M NOT. I'M JUST NOT SEEING A WHOLE LOT OF CHOICES.

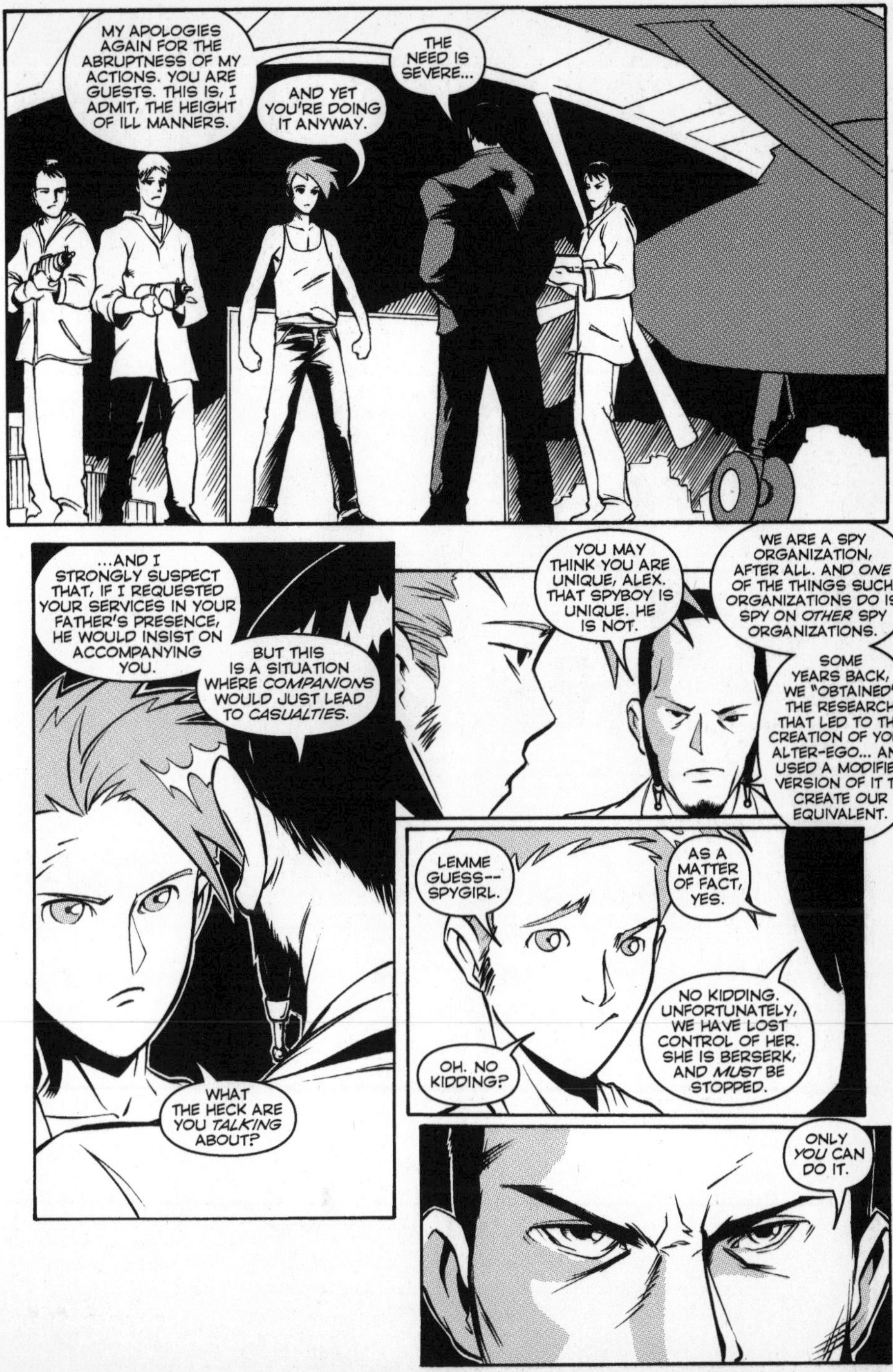

MY APOLOGIES AGAIN FOR THE ABRUPTNESS OF MY ACTIONS. YOU ARE GUESTS. THIS IS, I ADMIT, THE HEIGHT OF ILL MANNERS.
AND YET YOU'RE DOING IT ANYWAY.
THE NEED IS SEVERE...
...AND I STRONGLY SUSPECT THAT, IF I REQUESTED YOUR SERVICES IN YOUR FATHER'S PRESENCE, HE WOULD INSIST ON ACCOMPANYING YOU.
BUT THIS IS A SITUATION WHERE *COMPANIONS* WOULD JUST LEAD TO *CASUALTIES*.
WHAT THE HECK ARE YOU *TALKING* ABOUT?
YOU MAY THINK YOU ARE UNIQUE, ALEX. THAT SPYBOY IS UNIQUE. HE IS NOT.
WE ARE A SPY ORGANIZATION, AFTER ALL. AND *ONE* OF THE THINGS SUCH ORGANIZATIONS DO IS SPY ON *OTHER* SPY ORGANIZATIONS.
SOME YEARS BACK, WE "OBTAINED" THE RESEARCH THAT LED TO THE CREATION OF YOUR ALTER-EGO... AND USED A MODIFIED VERSION OF IT TO CREATE OUR EQUIVALENT.
LEMME GUESS-- SPYGIRL.
AS A MATTER OF FACT, YES.
OH. NO KIDDING?
NO KIDDING. UNFORTUNATELY, WE HAVE LOST CONTROL OF HER. SHE IS BERSERK, AND *MUST* BE STOPPED.
ONLY *YOU* CAN DO IT.

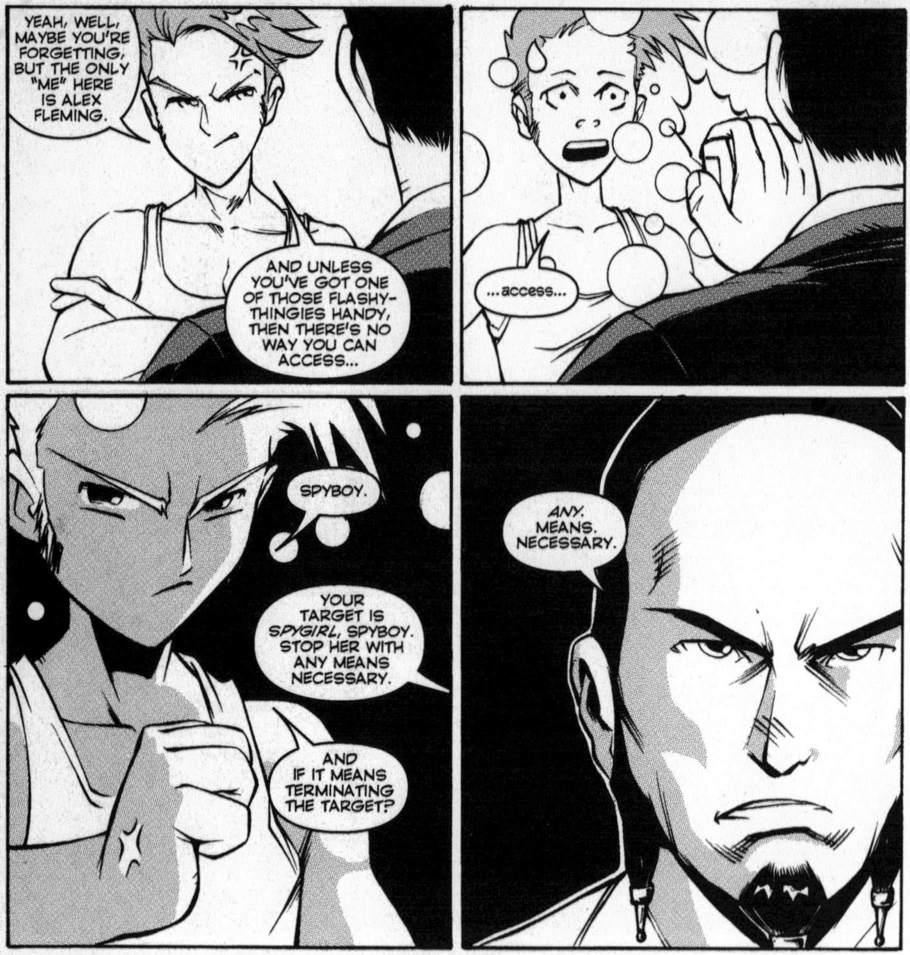
YEAH, WELL, MAYBE YOU'RE FORGETTING, BUT THE ONLY "ME" HERE IS ALEX FLEMING.
AND UNLESS YOU'VE GOT ONE OF THOSE FLASHY-THINGIES HANDY, THEN THERE'S NO WAY YOU CAN ACCESS...
...access...
SPYBOY.
YOUR TARGET IS *SPYGIRL*, SPYBOY. STOP HER WITH ANY MEANS NECESSARY.
AND IF IT MEANS TERMINATING THE TARGET?
ANY. MEANS. NECESSARY.

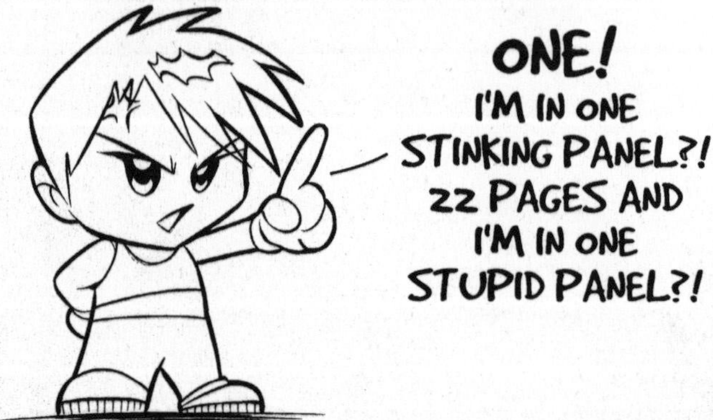
ONE!
I'M IN ONE STINKING PANEL?!
22 PAGES AND I'M IN ONE STUPID PANEL?!

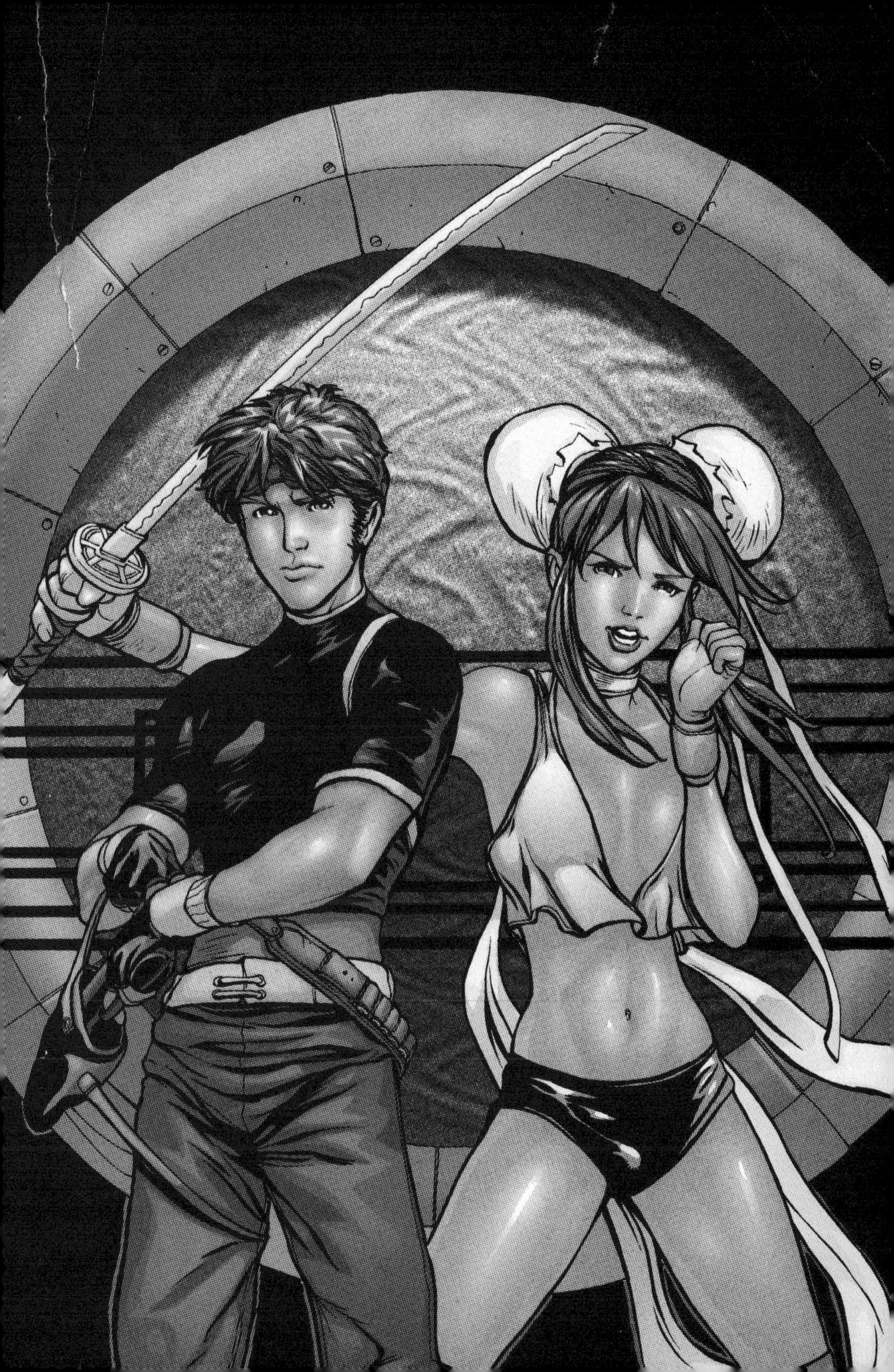

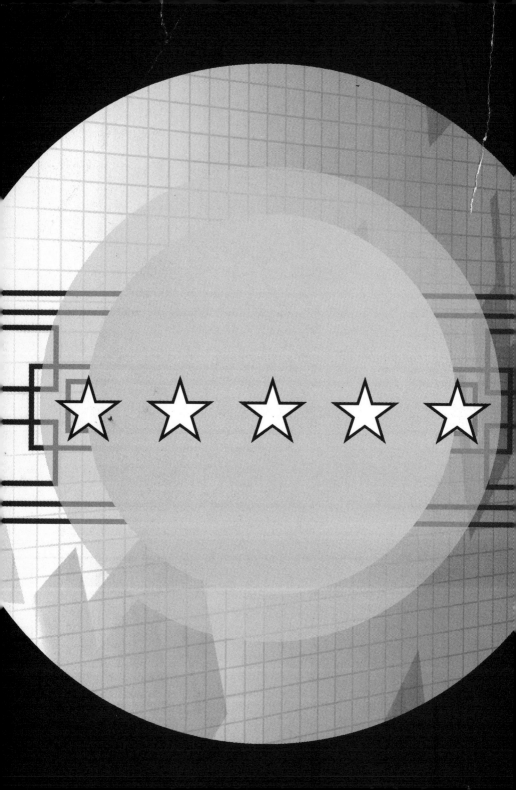

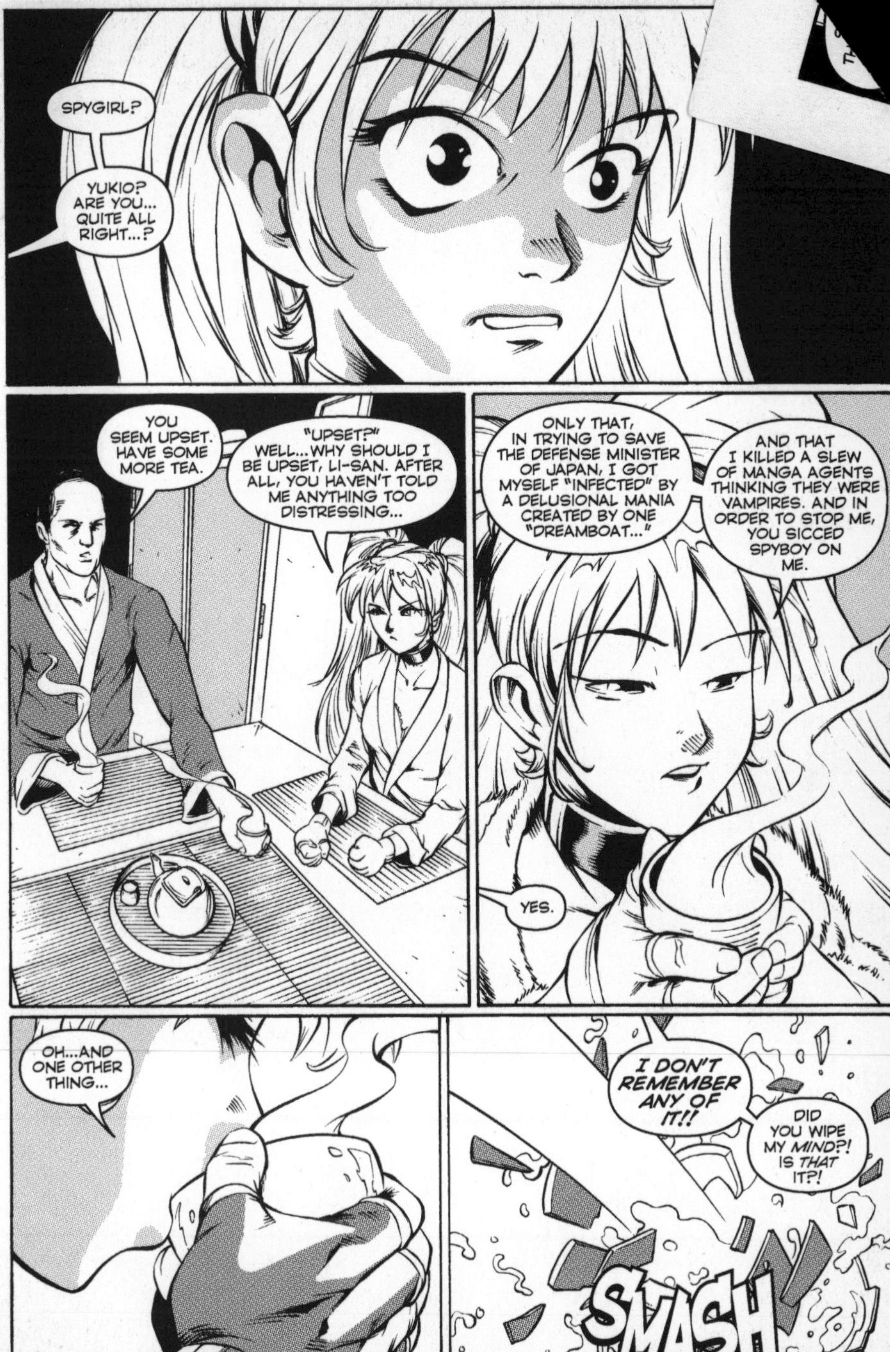
SPYGIRL?
YUKIO? ARE YOU... QUITE ALL RIGHT...?
YOU SEEM UPSET. HAVE SOME MORE TEA.
"UPSET?" WELL...WHY SHOULD I BE UPSET, LI-SAN. AFTER ALL, YOU HAVEN'T TOLD ME ANYTHING TOO DISTRESSING...
ONLY THAT, IN TRYING TO SAVE THE DEFENSE MINISTER OF JAPAN, I GOT MYSELF "INFECTED" BY A DELUSIONAL MANIA CREATED BY ONE "DREAMBOAT..."
AND THAT I KILLED A SLEW OF MANGA AGENTS THINKING THEY WERE VAMPIRES. AND IN ORDER TO STOP ME, YOU SICCED SPYBOY ON ME.
YES.
OH...AND ONE OTHER THING...
I DON'T REMEMBER ANY OF IT!!
DID YOU WIPE MY MIND?! IS THAT IT?!
SMASH

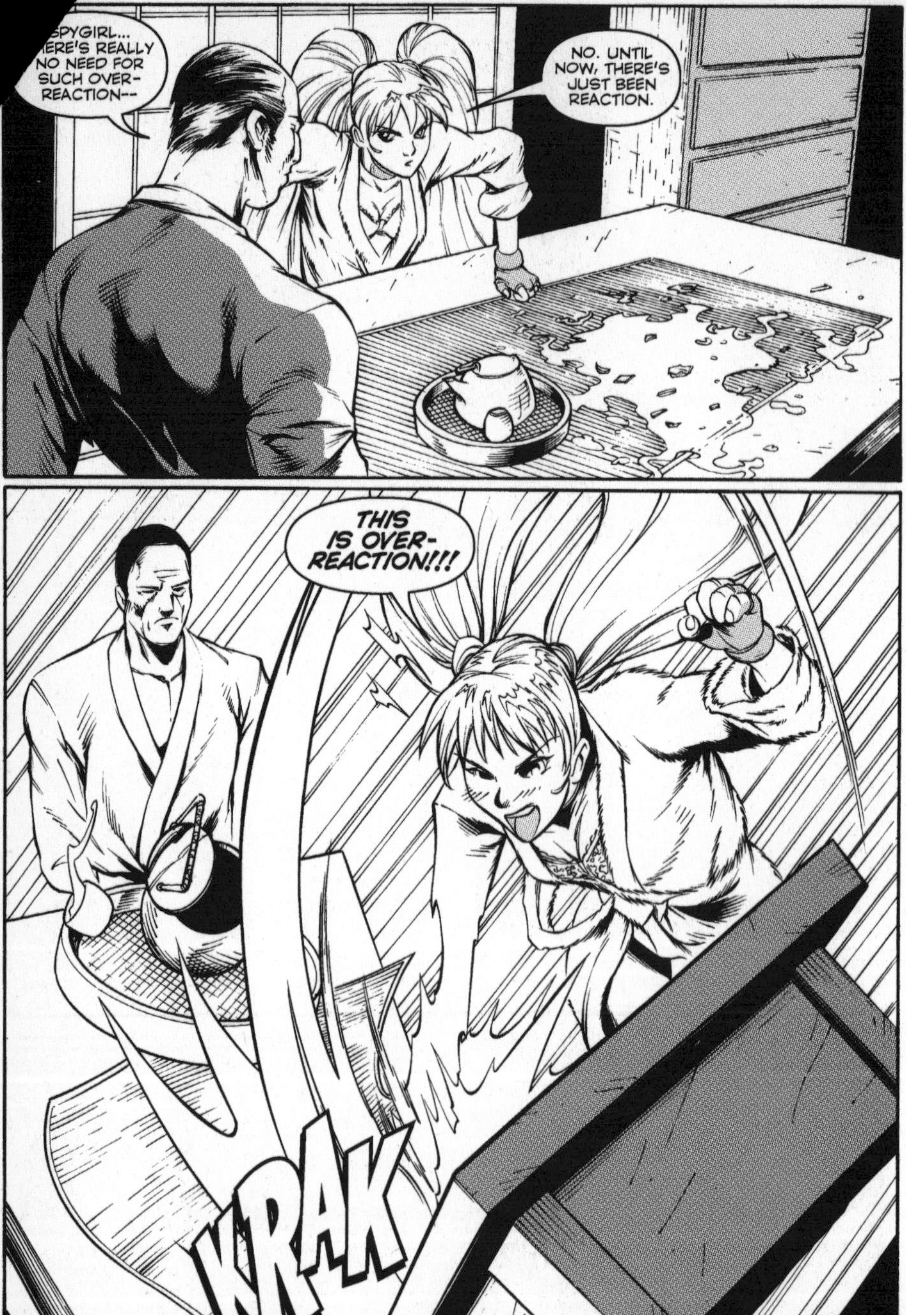
SPYGIRL... ERE'S REALLY NO NEED FOR SUCH OVER-REACTION--
NO. UNTIL NOW, THERE'S JUST BEEN REACTION.
THIS IS OVER-REACTION!!!
KRAK

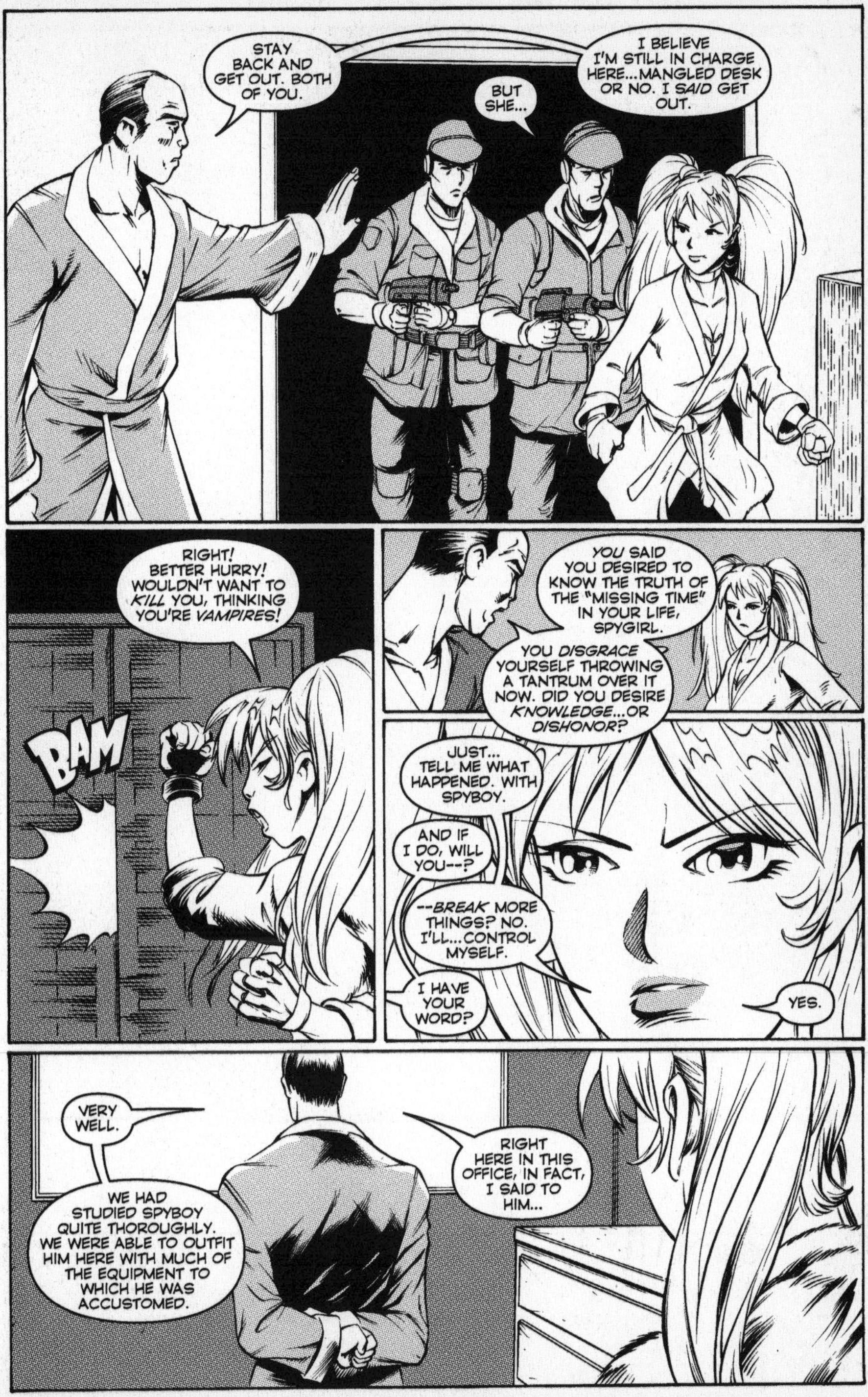
STAY BACK AND GET OUT. BOTH OF YOU.
BUT SHE...
I BELIEVE I'M STILL IN CHARGE HERE...MANGLED DESK OR NO. I *SAID* GET OUT.
RIGHT! BETTER HURRY! WOULDN'T WANT TO *KILL* YOU, THINKING YOU'RE *VAMPIRES*!
BAM
YOU SAID YOU DESIRED TO KNOW THE TRUTH OF THE "MISSING TIME" IN YOUR LIFE, SPYGIRL.
YOU *DISGRACE* YOURSELF THROWING A TANTRUM OVER IT NOW. DID YOU DESIRE *KNOWLEDGE*...OR *DISHONOR*?
JUST... TELL ME WHAT HAPPENED. WITH SPYBOY.
AND IF I DO, WILL YOU--?
--*BREAK* MORE THINGS? NO. I'LL...CONTROL MYSELF.
I HAVE YOUR WORD?
YES.
VERY WELL.
WE HAD STUDIED SPYBOY QUITE THOROUGHLY. WE WERE ABLE TO OUTFIT HIM HERE WITH MUCH OF THE EQUIPMENT TO WHICH HE WAS ACCUSTOMED.
RIGHT HERE IN THIS OFFICE, IN FACT, I SAID TO HIM...

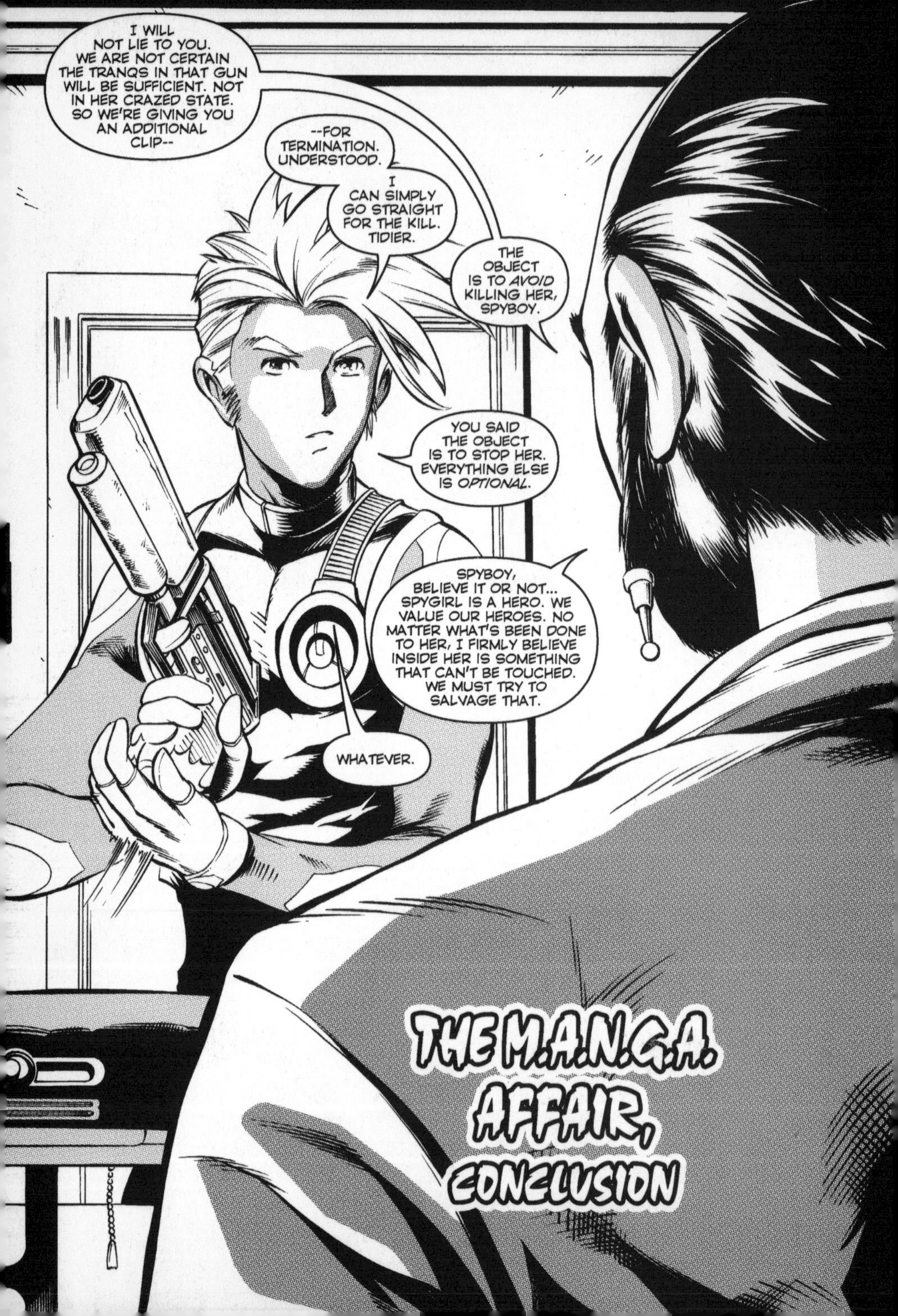
I WILL NOT LIE TO YOU. WE ARE NOT CERTAIN THE TRANQS IN THAT GUN WILL BE SUFFICIENT. NOT IN HER CRAZED STATE. SO WE'RE GIVING YOU AN ADDITIONAL CLIP--
--FOR TERMINATION. UNDERSTOOD.
I CAN SIMPLY GO STRAIGHT FOR THE KILL. TIDIER.
THE OBJECT IS TO *AVOID* KILLING HER, SPYBOY.
YOU SAID THE OBJECT IS TO STOP HER. EVERYTHING ELSE IS *OPTIONAL*.
SPYBOY, BELIEVE IT OR NOT... SPYGIRL IS A HERO. WE VALUE OUR HEROES. NO MATTER WHAT'S BEEN DONE TO HER, I FIRMLY BELIEVE INSIDE HER IS SOMETHING THAT CAN'T BE TOUCHED. WE MUST TRY TO SALVAGE THAT.
WHATEVER.
THE M.A.N.G.A. AFFAIR, CONCLUSION

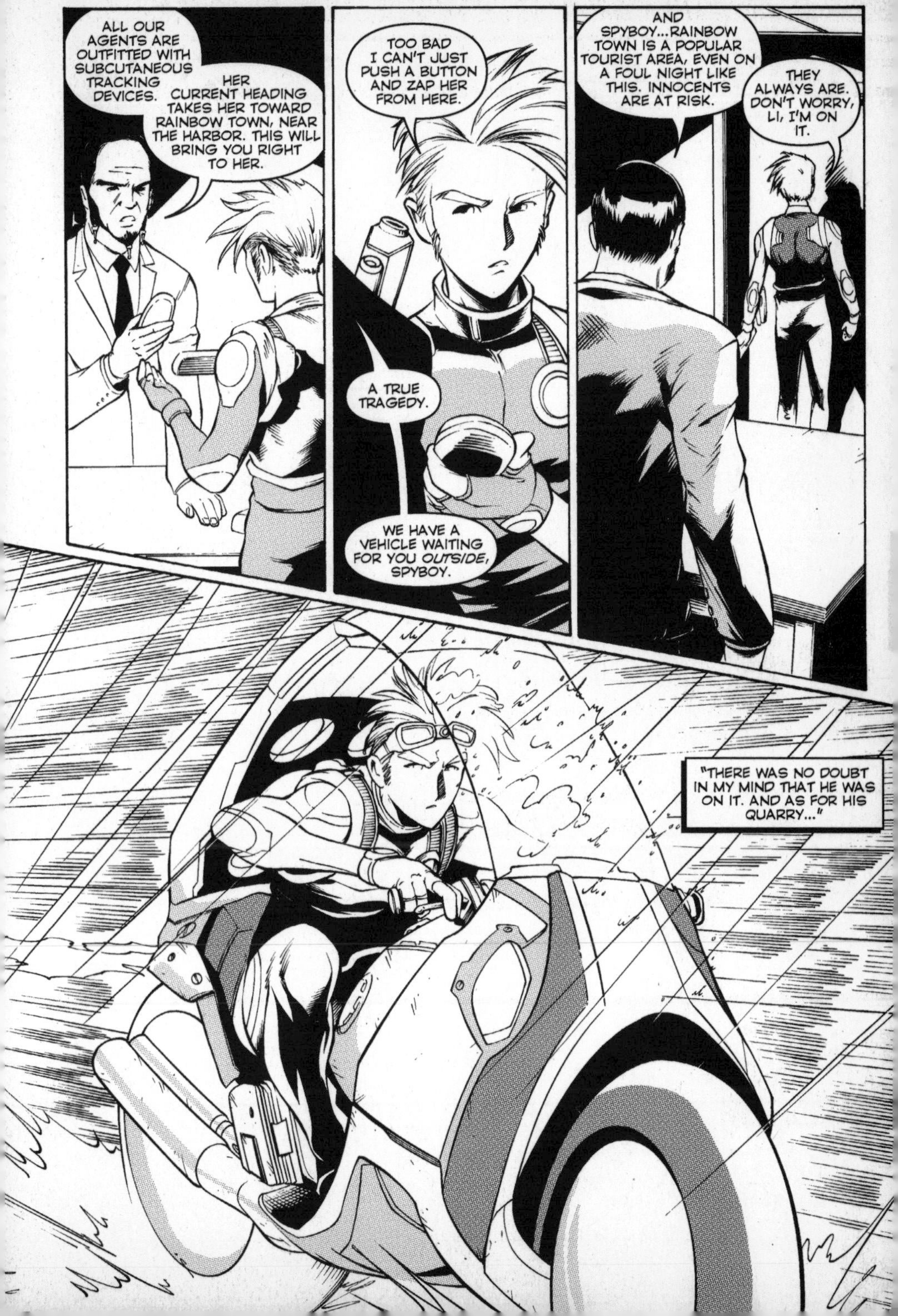
ALL OUR AGENTS ARE OUTFITTED WITH SUBCUTANEOUS TRACKING DEVICES.
HER CURRENT HEADING TAKES HER TOWARD RAINBOW TOWN, NEAR THE HARBOR. THIS WILL BRING YOU RIGHT TO HER.
TOO BAD I CAN'T JUST PUSH A BUTTON AND ZAP HER FROM HERE.
A TRUE TRAGEDY.
WE HAVE A VEHICLE WAITING FOR YOU *OUTSIDE*, SPYBOY.
AND SPYBOY...RAINBOW TOWN IS A POPULAR TOURIST AREA, EVEN ON A FOUL NIGHT LIKE THIS. INNOCENTS ARE AT RISK.
THEY ALWAYS ARE. DON'T WORRY, LI, I'M ON IT.
"THERE WAS NO DOUBT IN MY MIND THAT HE WAS ON IT. AND AS FOR HIS QUARRY..."

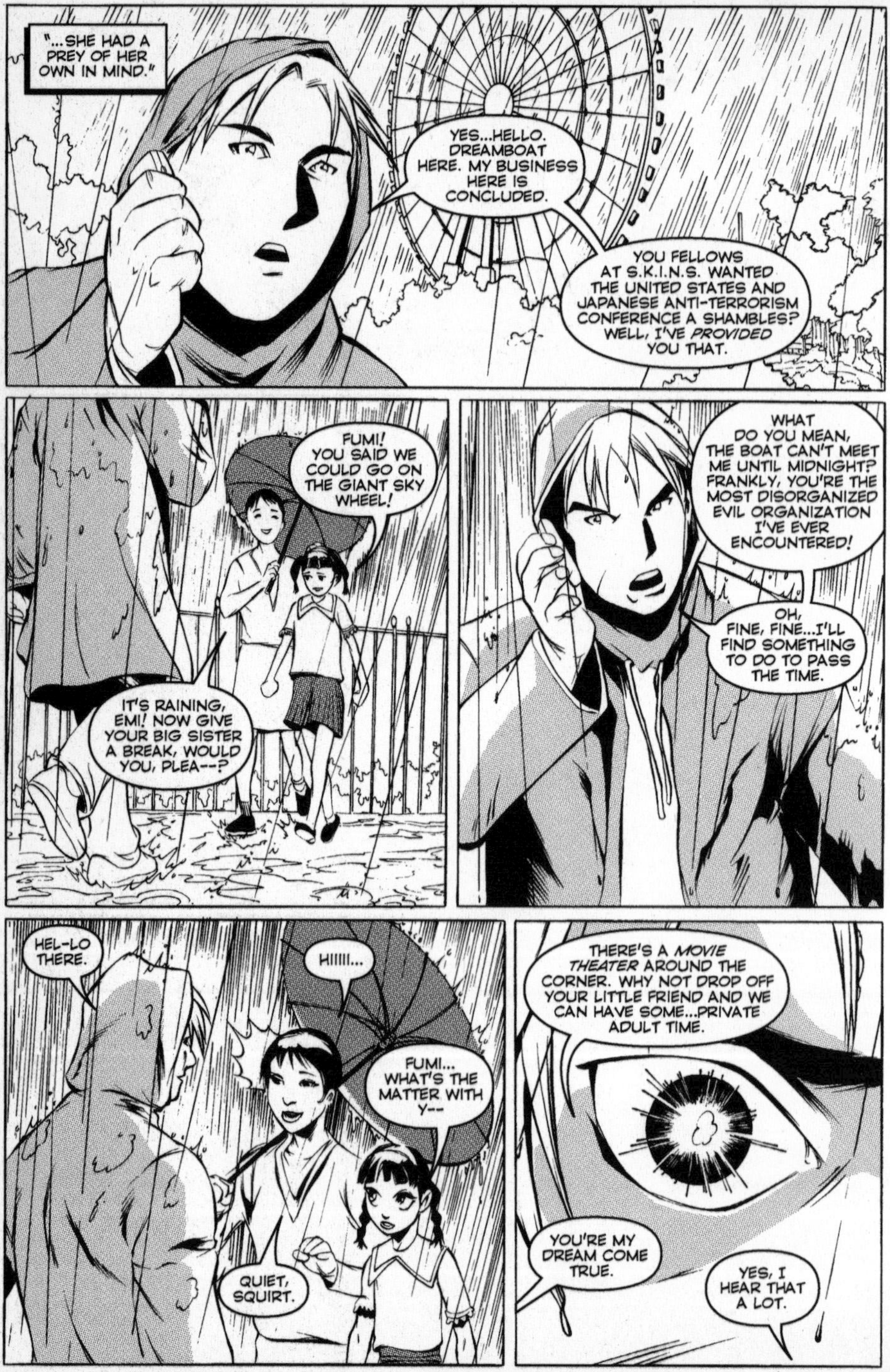
"...SHE HAD A PREY OF HER OWN IN MIND."
YES...HELLO. DREAMBOAT HERE. MY BUSINESS HERE IS CONCLUDED.
YOU FELLOWS AT S.K.I.N.S. WANTED THE UNITED STATES AND JAPANESE ANTI-TERRORISM CONFERENCE A SHAMBLES? WELL, I'VE *PROVIDED* YOU THAT.
FUMI! YOU SAID WE COULD GO ON THE GIANT SKY WHEEL!
IT'S RAINING, EMI! NOW GIVE YOUR BIG SISTER A BREAK, WOULD YOU, PLEA--?
WHAT DO YOU MEAN, THE BOAT CAN'T MEET ME UNTIL MIDNIGHT? FRANKLY, YOU'RE THE MOST DISORGANIZED EVIL ORGANIZATION I'VE EVER ENCOUNTERED!
OH, FINE, FINE...I'LL FIND SOMETHING TO DO TO PASS THE TIME.
HEL-LO THERE.
HIIIII...
FUMI... WHAT'S THE MATTER WITH Y--
QUIET, SQUIRT.
THERE'S A *MOVIE THEATER* AROUND THE CORNER. WHY NOT DROP OFF YOUR LITTLE FRIEND AND WE CAN HAVE SOME...PRIVATE ADULT TIME.
YOU'RE MY DREAM COME TRUE.
YES, I HEAR THAT A LOT.

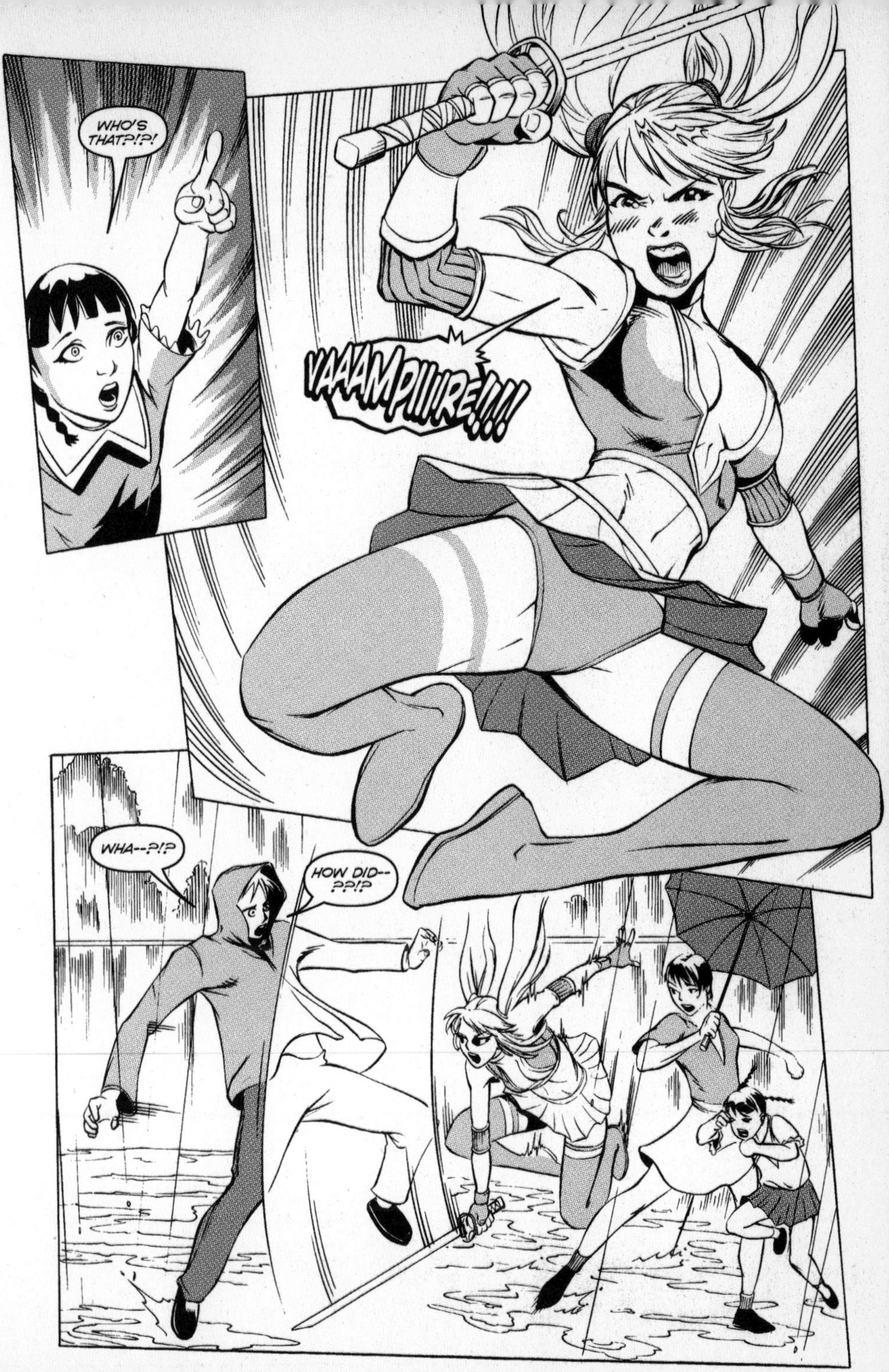
WHO'S THAT?!?!
VAAAMPIIIRE!!!!
WHA--?!?
HOW DID-- ??!?

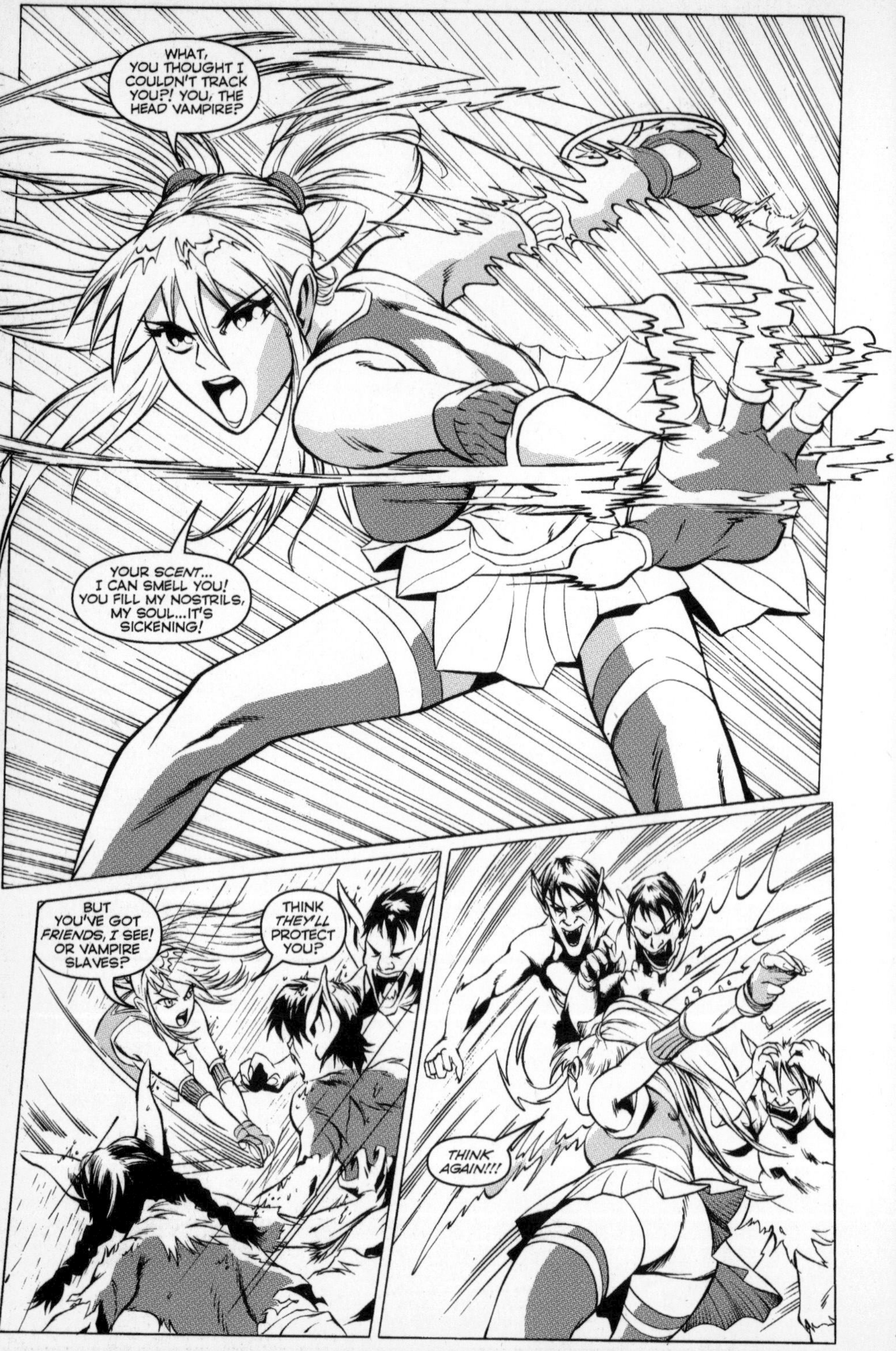
WHAT, YOU THOUGHT I COULDN'T TRACK YOU?! YOU, THE HEAD VAMPIRE?
YOUR SCENT... I CAN SMELL YOU! YOU FILL MY NOSTRILS, MY SOUL...IT'S SICKENING!
BUT YOU'VE GOT FRIENDS, I SEE! OR VAMPIRE SLAVES?
THINK THEY'LL PROTECT YOU?
THINK AGAIN!!!

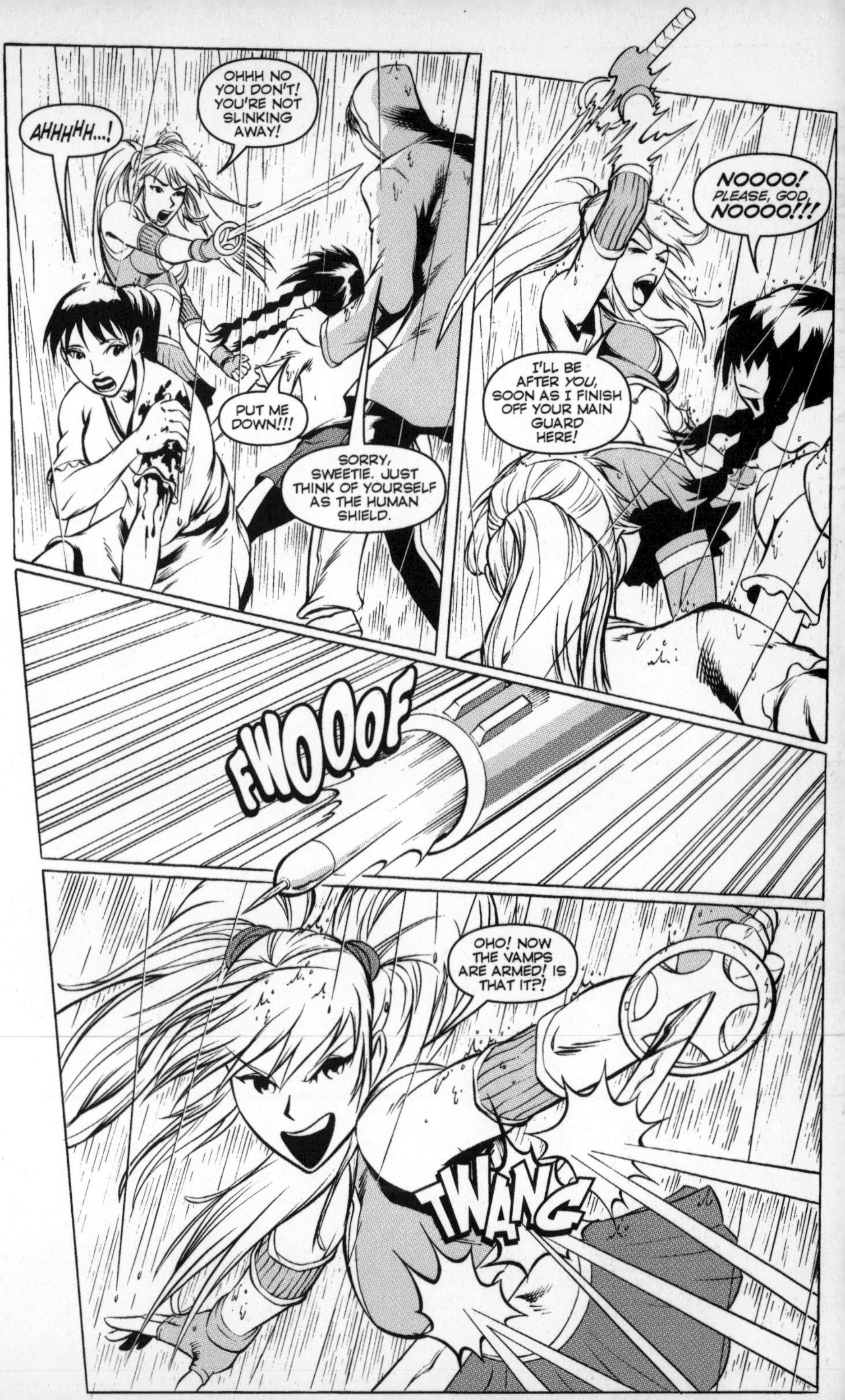
AHHHHH...!
OHHH NO YOU DON'T! YOU'RE NOT SLINKING AWAY!
PUT ME DOWN!!!
SORRY, SWEETIE. JUST THINK OF YOURSELF AS THE HUMAN SHIELD.
NOOOO! PLEASE, GOD NOOOO!!!
I'LL BE AFTER YOU, SOON AS I FINISH OFF YOUR MAIN GUARD HERE!
FWOOOF
OHO! NOW THE VAMPS ARE ARMED! IS THAT IT?!
TWANG

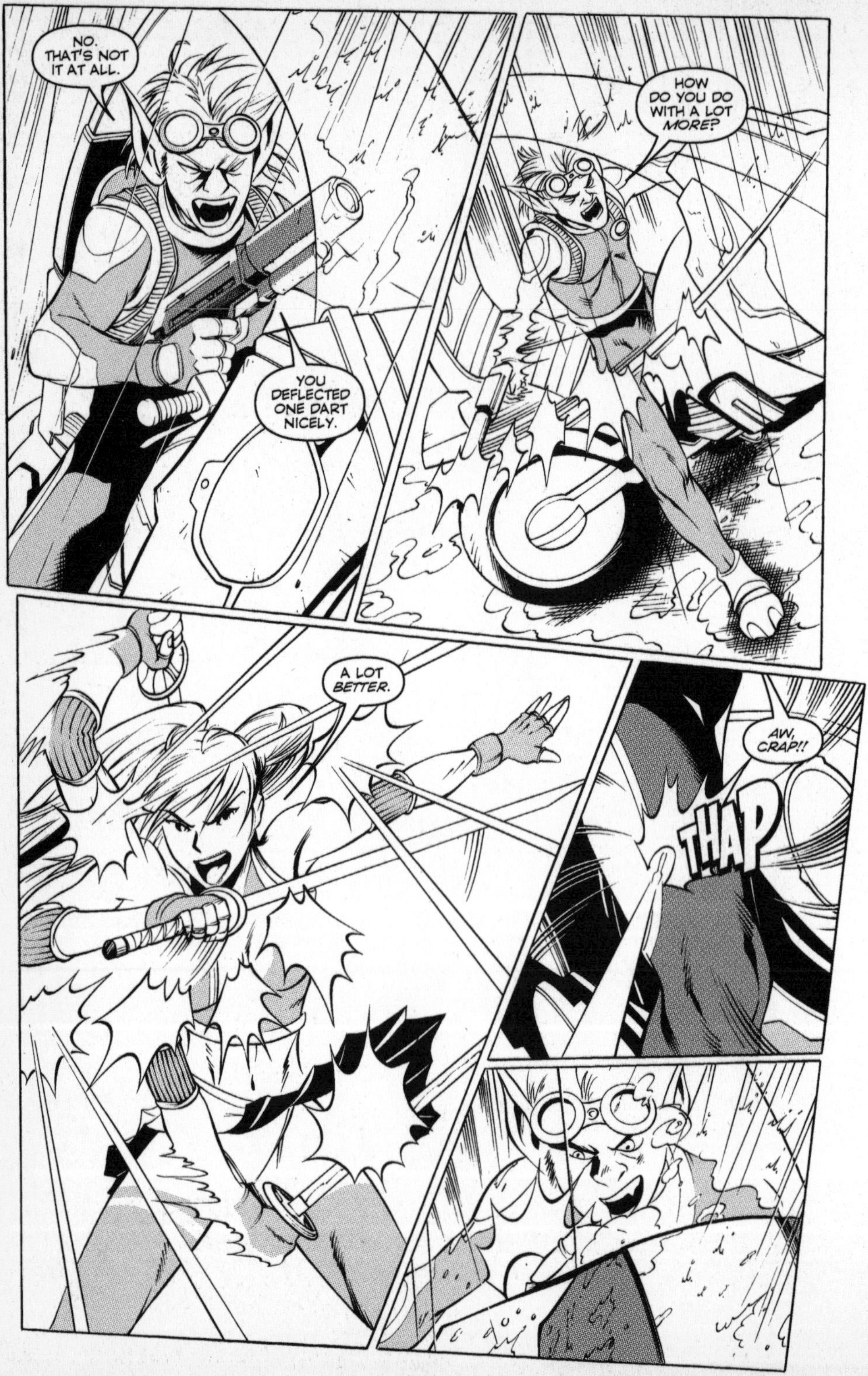
NO. THAT'S NOT IT AT ALL.
YOU DEFLECTED ONE DART NICELY.
HOW DO YOU DO WITH A LOT *MORE?*
A LOT *BETTER.*
AW, CRAP!!
THAP

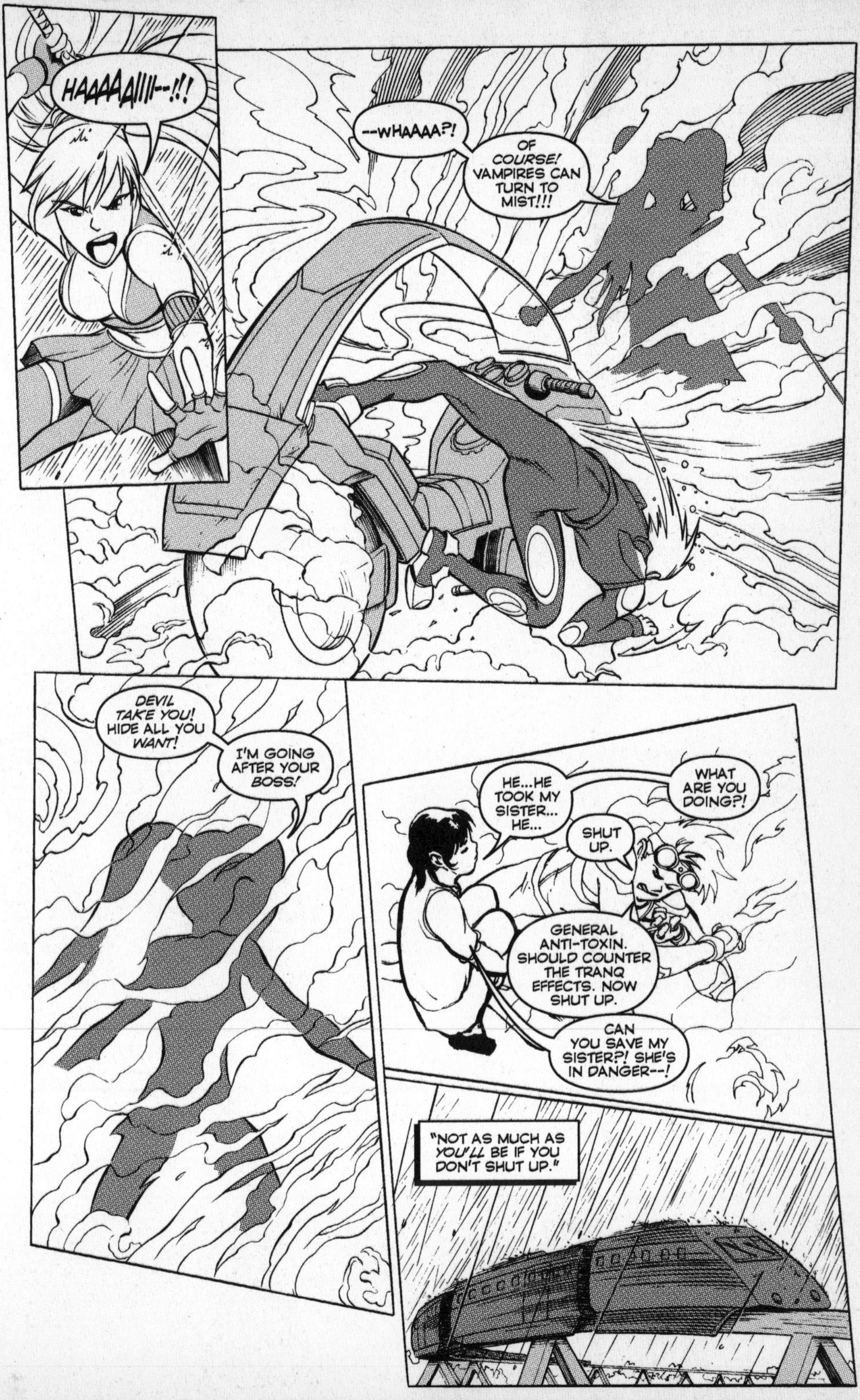
HAAAAAIIII--!!!
--WHAAAA?!
OF COURSE! VAMPIRES CAN TURN TO MIST!!!
DEVIL TAKE YOU! HIDE ALL YOU WANT!
I'M GOING AFTER YOUR BOSS!
HE...HE TOOK MY SISTER... HE...
WHAT ARE YOU DOING?!
SHUT UP.
GENERAL ANTI-TOXIN. SHOULD COUNTER THE TRANQ EFFECTS. NOW SHUT UP.
CAN YOU SAVE MY SISTER?! SHE'S IN DANGER--!
"NOT AS MUCH AS YOU'LL BE IF YOU DON'T SHUT UP."

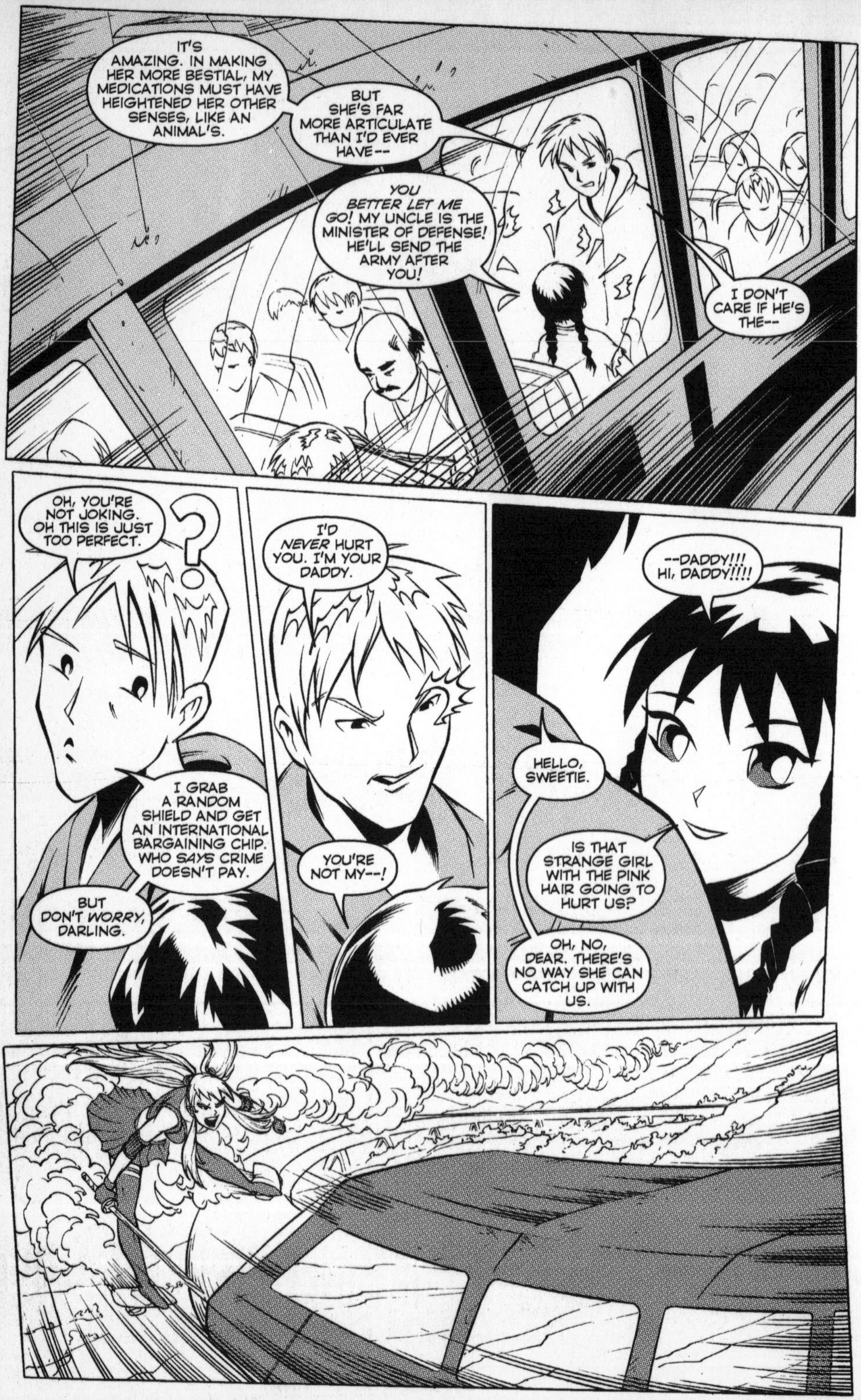
IT'S AMAZING. IN MAKING HER MORE BESTIAL, MY MEDICATIONS MUST HAVE HEIGHTENED HER OTHER SENSES, LIKE AN ANIMAL'S.
BUT SHE'S FAR MORE ARTICULATE THAN I'D EVER HAVE--
YOU BETTER LET ME GO! MY UNCLE IS THE MINISTER OF DEFENSE! HE'LL SEND THE ARMY AFTER YOU!
I DON'T CARE IF HE'S THE--
OH, YOU'RE NOT JOKING. OH THIS IS JUST TOO PERFECT.
?
I GRAB A RANDOM SHIELD AND GET AN INTERNATIONAL BARGAINING CHIP. WHO SAYS CRIME DOESN'T PAY.
BUT DON'T WORRY, DARLING.
I'D NEVER HURT YOU. I'M YOUR DADDY.
YOU'RE NOT MY--!
--DADDY!!! HI, DADDY!!!!
HELLO, SWEETIE.
IS THAT STRANGE GIRL WITH THE PINK HAIR GOING TO HURT US?
OH, NO, DEAR. THERE'S NO WAY SHE CAN CATCH UP WITH US.

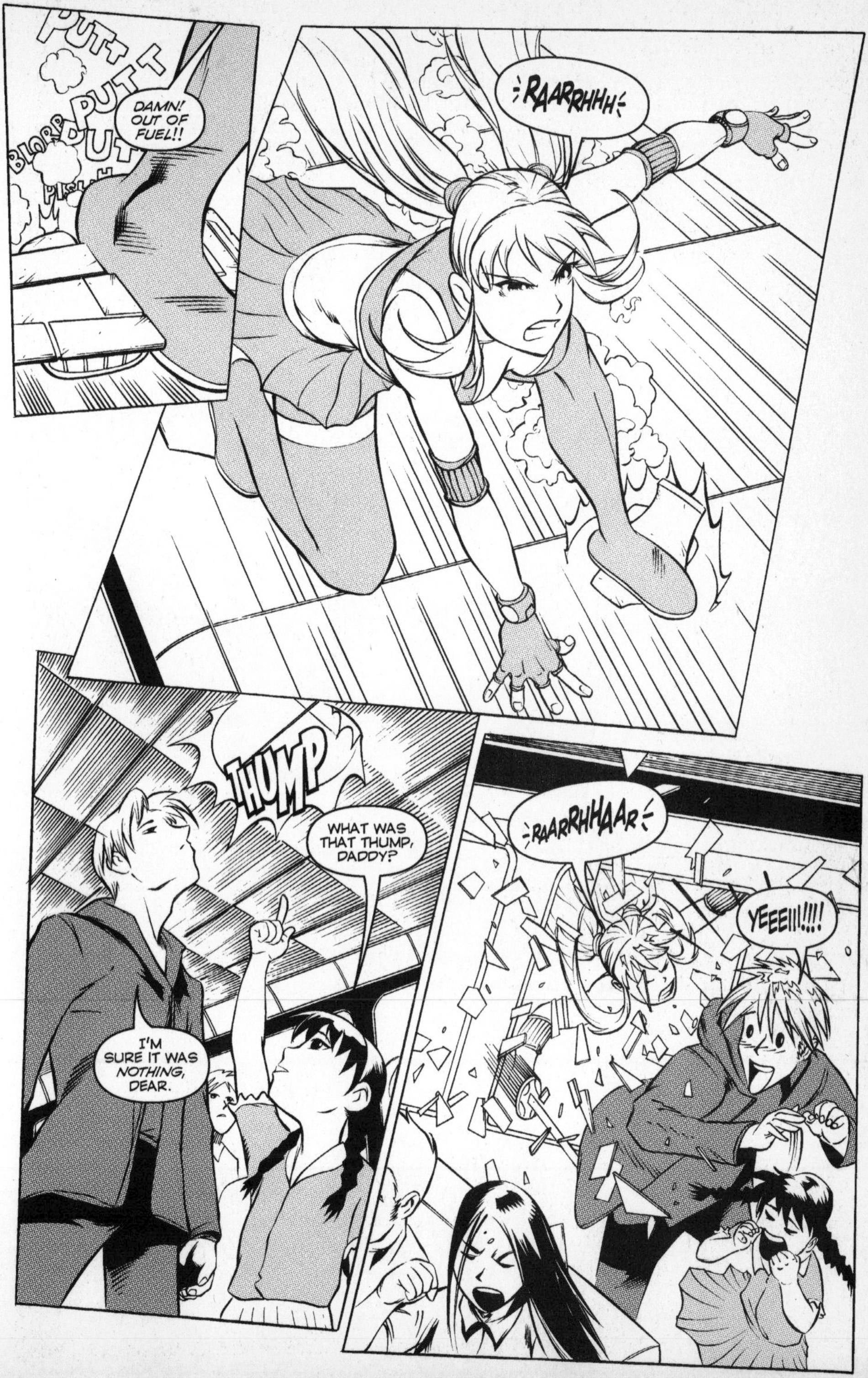
PUTT
PUTT
BLORP
DUTT
DAMN! OUT OF FUEL!!
RAARRHHH
THUMP
WHAT WAS THAT THUMP, DADDY?
I'M SURE IT WAS *NOTHING*, DEAR.
RAARRHHAAR
YEEII!!!!

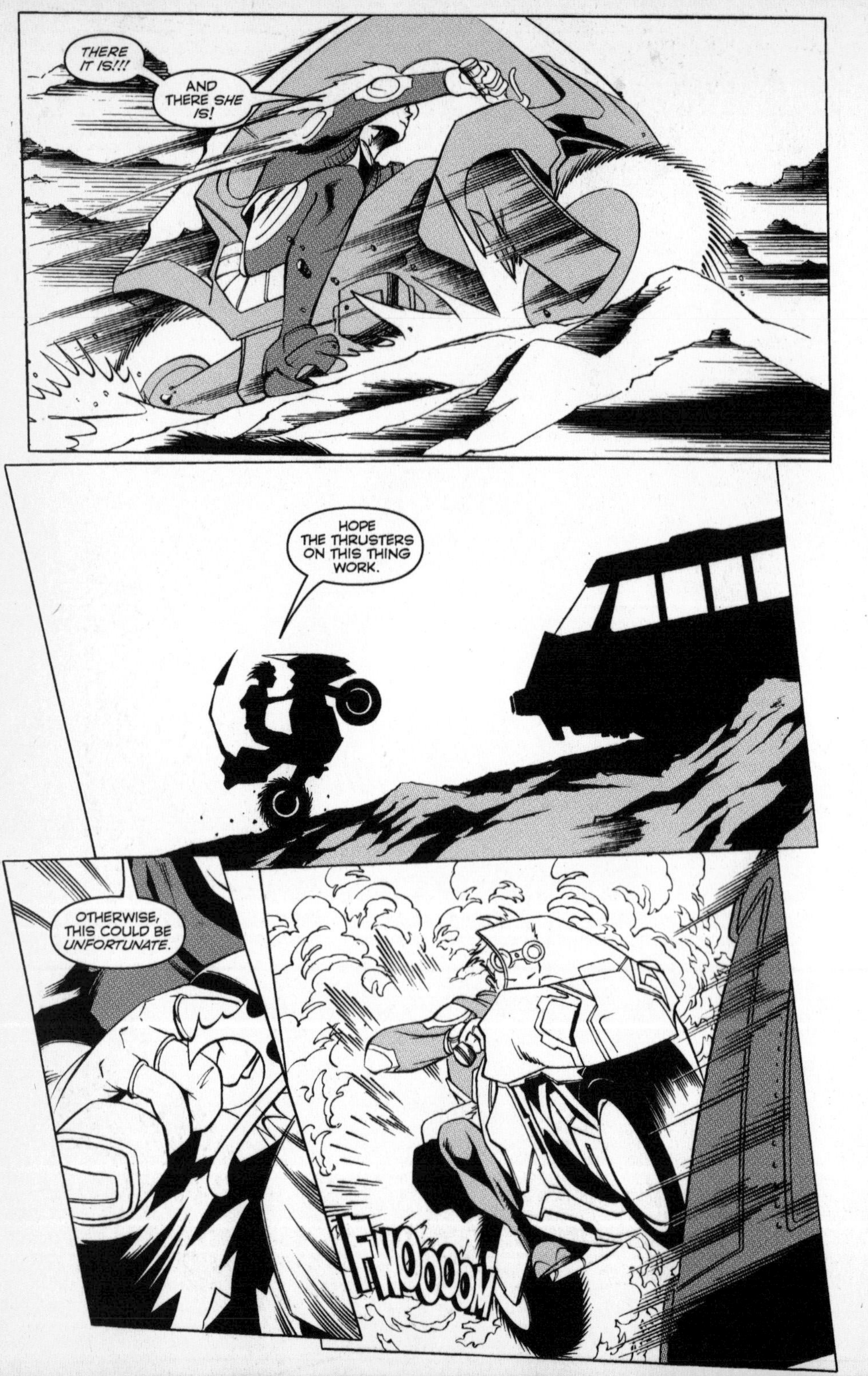

THERE IT IS!!!
AND THERE SHE IS!
HOPE THE THRUSTERS ON THIS THING WORK.
OTHERWISE, THIS COULD BE UNFORTUNATE.
FWOOOOM

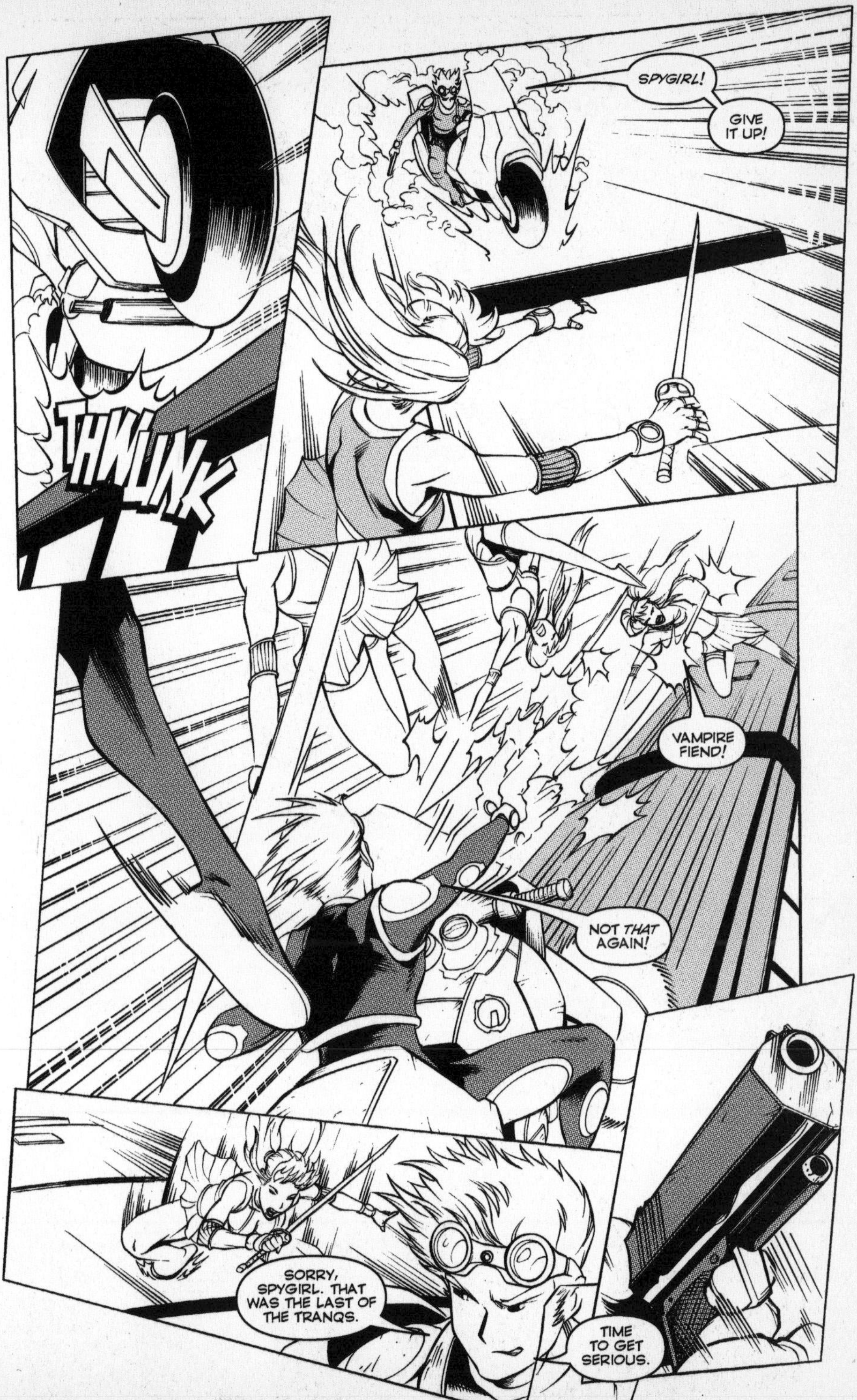
SPYGIRL!
GIVE IT UP!
THWUNK
VAMPIRE FIEND!
NOT THAT AGAIN!
SORRY, SPYGIRL. THAT WAS THE LAST OF THE TRANQS.
TIME TO GET SERIOUS.

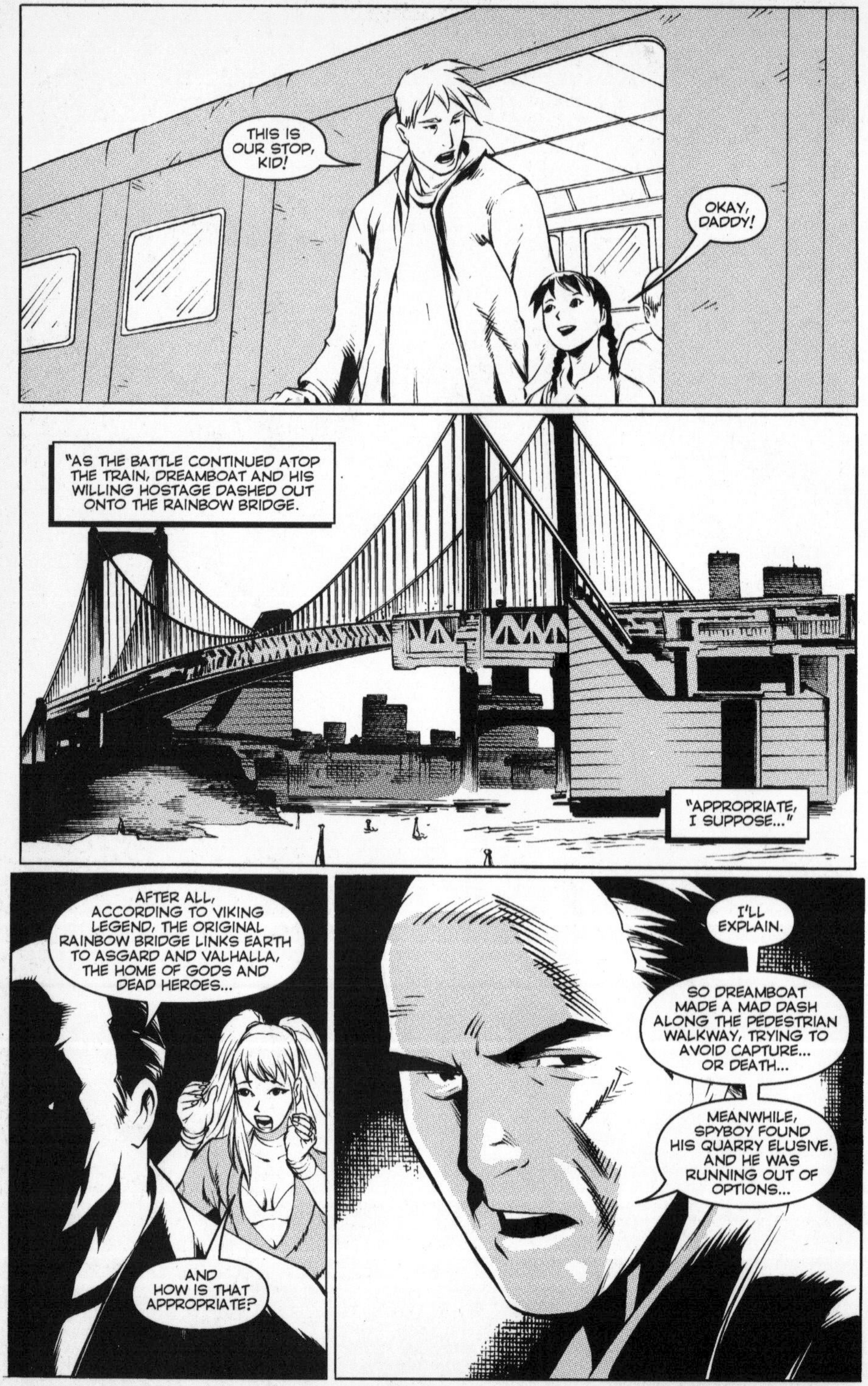
THIS IS OUR STOP, KID!
OKAY, DADDY!
"AS THE BATTLE CONTINUED ATOP THE TRAIN, DREAMBOAT AND HIS WILLING HOSTAGE DASHED OUT ONTO THE RAINBOW BRIDGE.
"APPROPRIATE, I SUPPOSE..."
AFTER ALL, ACCORDING TO VIKING LEGEND, THE ORIGINAL RAINBOW BRIDGE LINKS EARTH TO ASGARD AND VALHALLA, THE HOME OF GODS AND DEAD HEROES...
AND HOW IS THAT APPROPRIATE?
I'LL EXPLAIN.
SO DREAMBOAT MADE A MAD DASH ALONG THE PEDESTRIAN WALKWAY, TRYING TO AVOID CAPTURE... OR DEATH...
MEANWHILE, SPYBOY FOUND HIS QUARRY ELUSIVE. AND HE WAS RUNNING OUT OF OPTIONS...

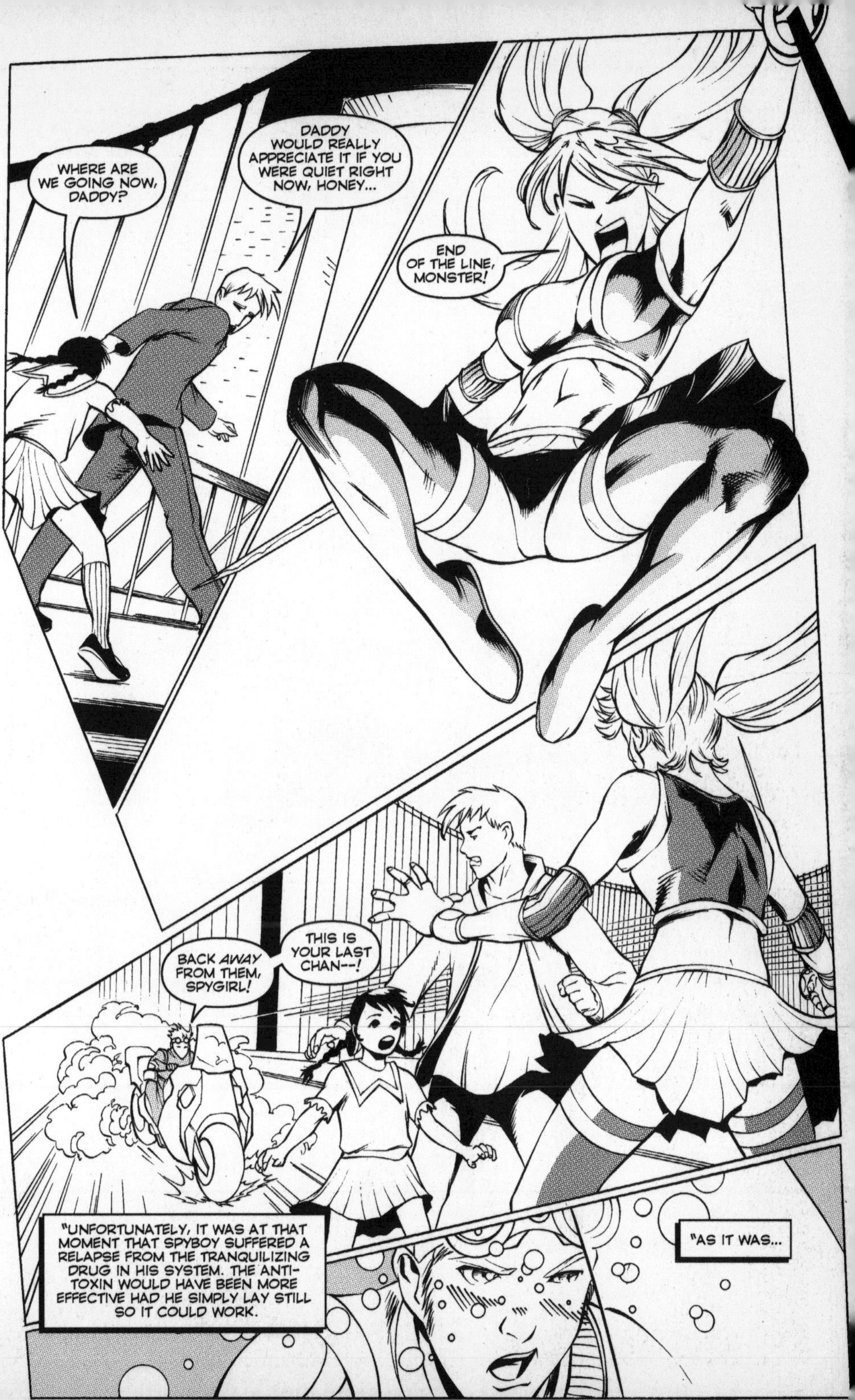
WHERE ARE WE GOING NOW, DADDY?
DADDY WOULD REALLY APPRECIATE IT IF YOU WERE QUIET RIGHT NOW, HONEY...
END OF THE LINE, MONSTER!
BACK AWAY FROM THEM, SPYGIRL!
THIS IS YOUR LAST CHAN--!
"UNFORTUNATELY, IT WAS AT THAT MOMENT THAT SPYBOY SUFFERED A RELAPSE FROM THE TRANQUILIZING DRUG IN HIS SYSTEM. THE ANTI-TOXIN WOULD HAVE BEEN MORE EFFECTIVE HAD HE SIMPLY LAY STILL SO IT COULD WORK.
"AS IT WAS...

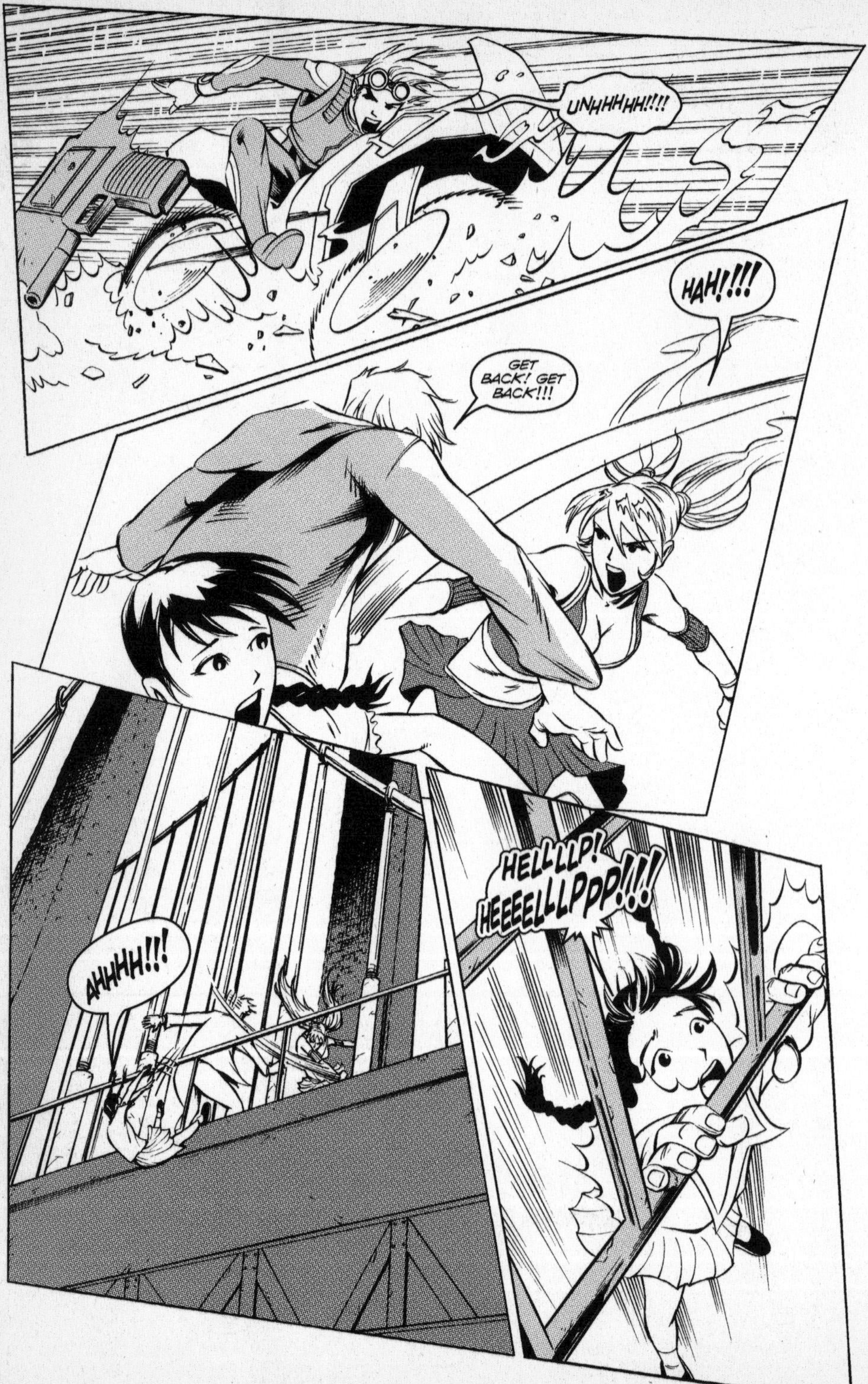
UNHHHHH!!!!
HAH!!!!
GET BACK! GET BACK!!!
AHHHH!!!
HELLLLP! HEEEELLLPPP!!!

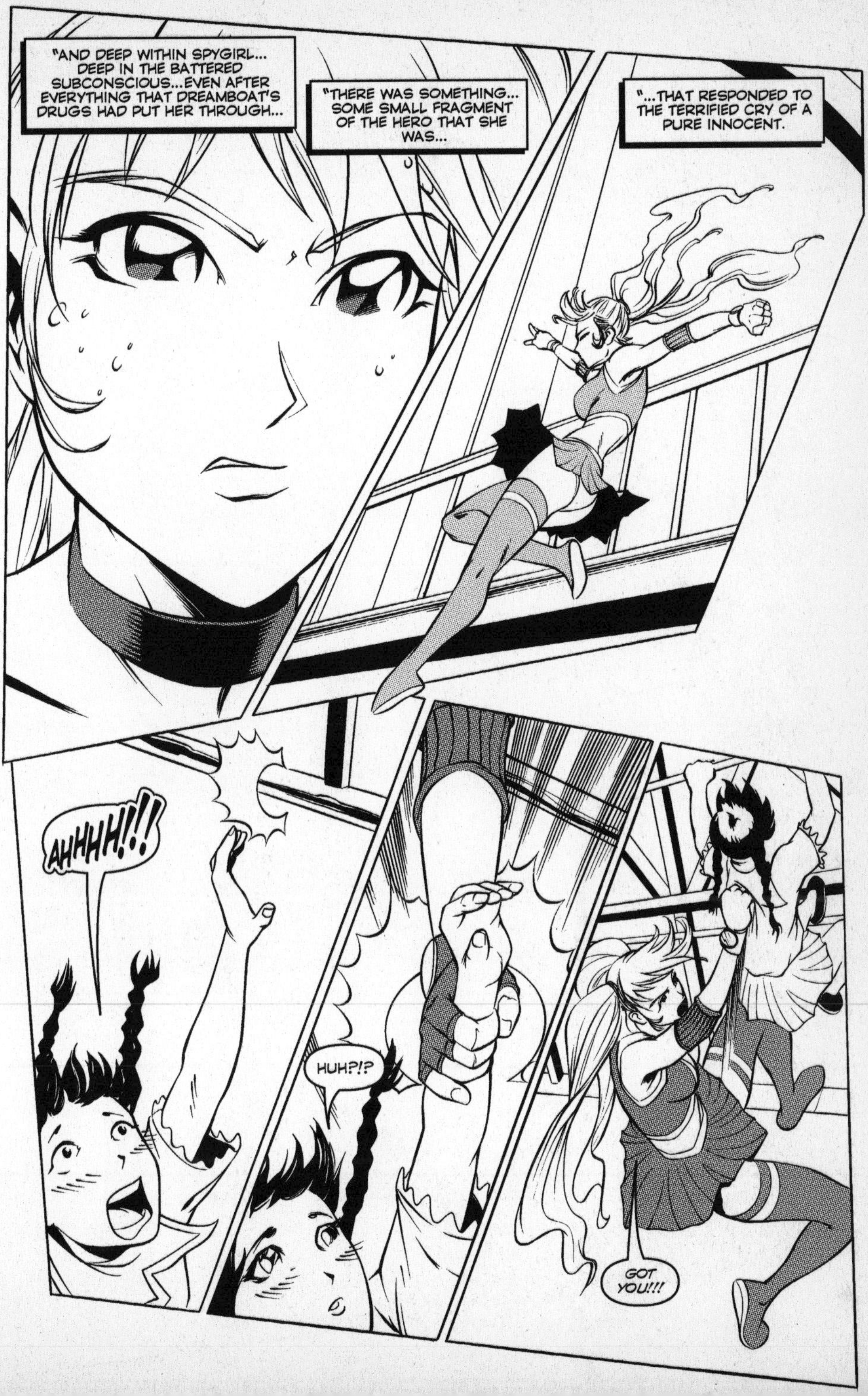
"AND DEEP WITHIN SPYGIRL... DEEP IN THE BATTERED SUBCONSCIOUS...EVEN AFTER EVERYTHING THAT DREAMBOAT'S DRUGS HAD PUT HER THROUGH...
"THERE WAS SOMETHING... SOME SMALL FRAGMENT OF THE HERO THAT SHE WAS...
"...THAT RESPONDED TO THE TERRIFIED CRY OF A PURE INNOCENT.
AHHHH!!!
HUH?!?
GOT YOU!!!

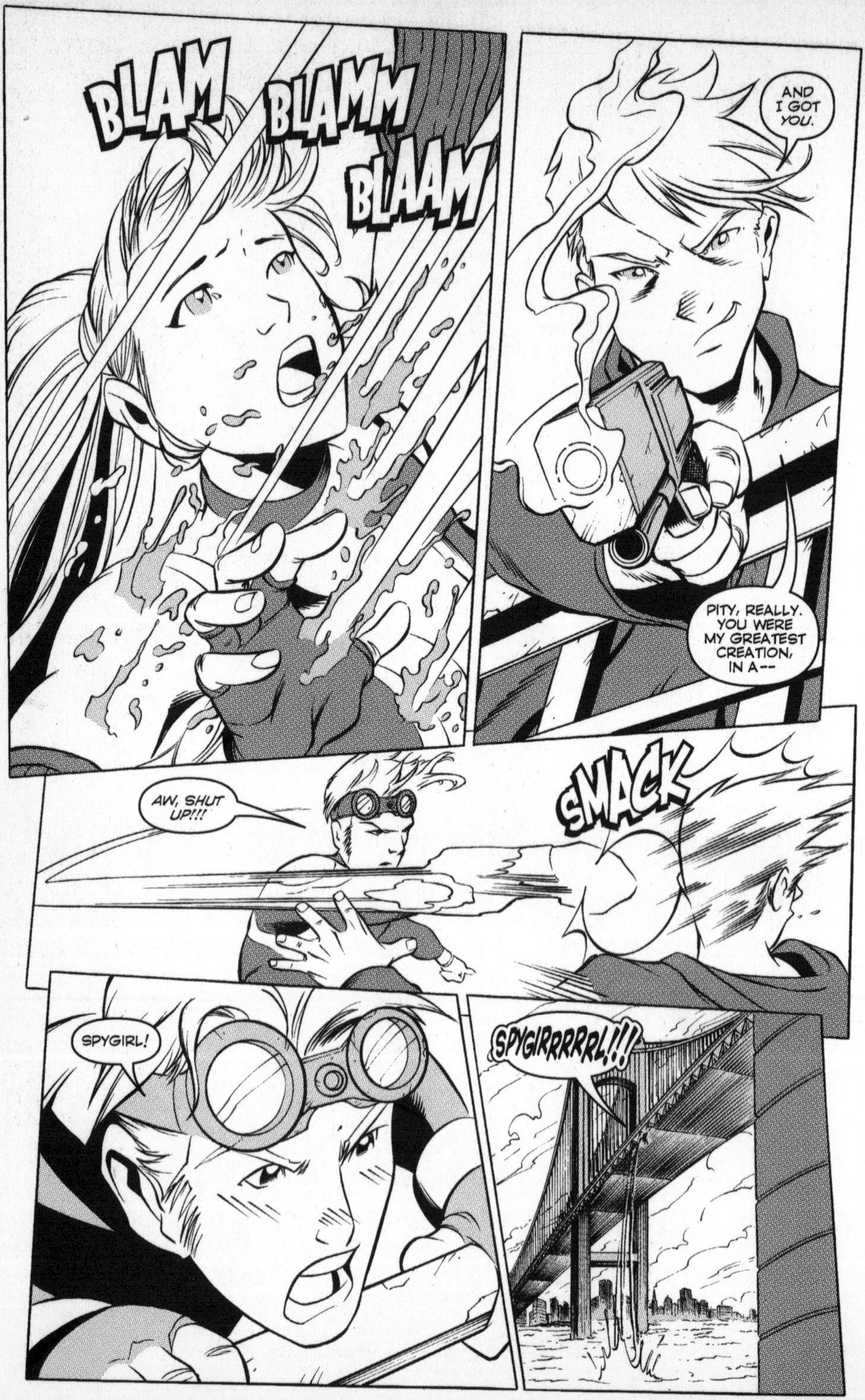
BLAM
BLAMM
BLAAM
AND I GOT YOU.
PITY, REALLY. YOU WERE MY GREATEST CREATION, IN A--
AW, SHUT UP!!!
SMACK
SPYGIRL!
SPYGIRRRRRL!!!

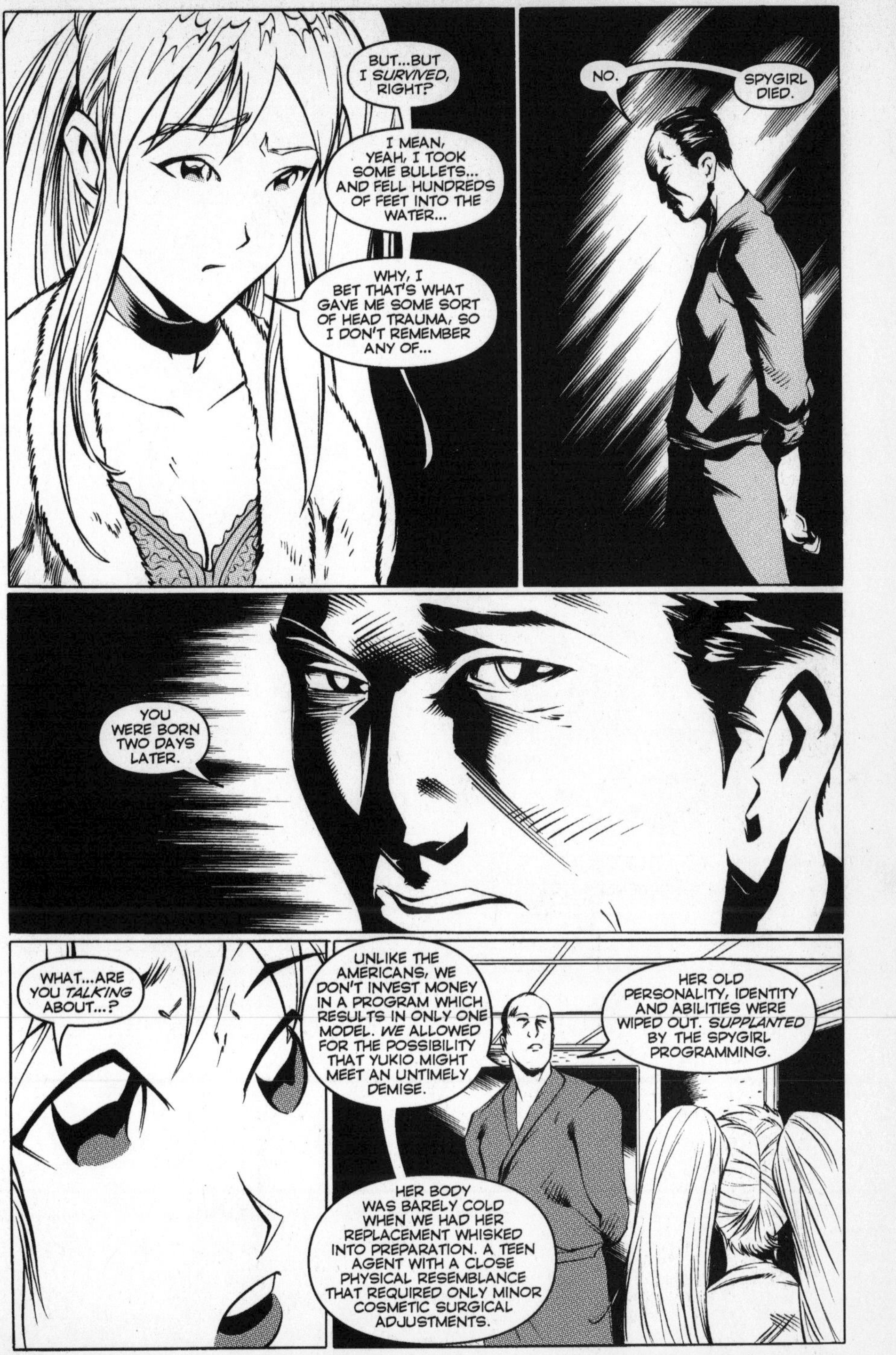
BUT...BUT I *SURVIVED,* RIGHT?
I MEAN, YEAH, I TOOK SOME BULLETS... AND FELL HUNDREDS OF FEET INTO THE WATER...
WHY, I BET THAT'S WHAT GAVE ME SOME SORT OF HEAD TRAUMA, SO I DON'T REMEMBER ANY OF...
NO.
SPYGIRL DIED.
YOU WERE BORN TWO DAYS LATER.
WHAT...ARE YOU *TALKING* ABOUT...?
UNLIKE THE AMERICANS, WE DON'T INVEST MONEY IN A PROGRAM WHICH RESULTS IN ONLY ONE MODEL. *WE* ALLOWED FOR THE POSSIBILITY THAT YUKIO MIGHT MEET AN UNTIMELY DEMISE.
HER BODY WAS BARELY COLD WHEN WE HAD HER REPLACEMENT WHISKED INTO PREPARATION. A TEEN AGENT WITH A CLOSE PHYSICAL RESEMBLANCE THAT REQUIRED ONLY MINOR COSMETIC SURGICAL ADJUSTMENTS.
HER OLD PERSONALITY, IDENTITY AND ABILITIES WERE WIPED OUT. *SUPPLANTED* BY THE SPYGIRL PROGRAMMING.

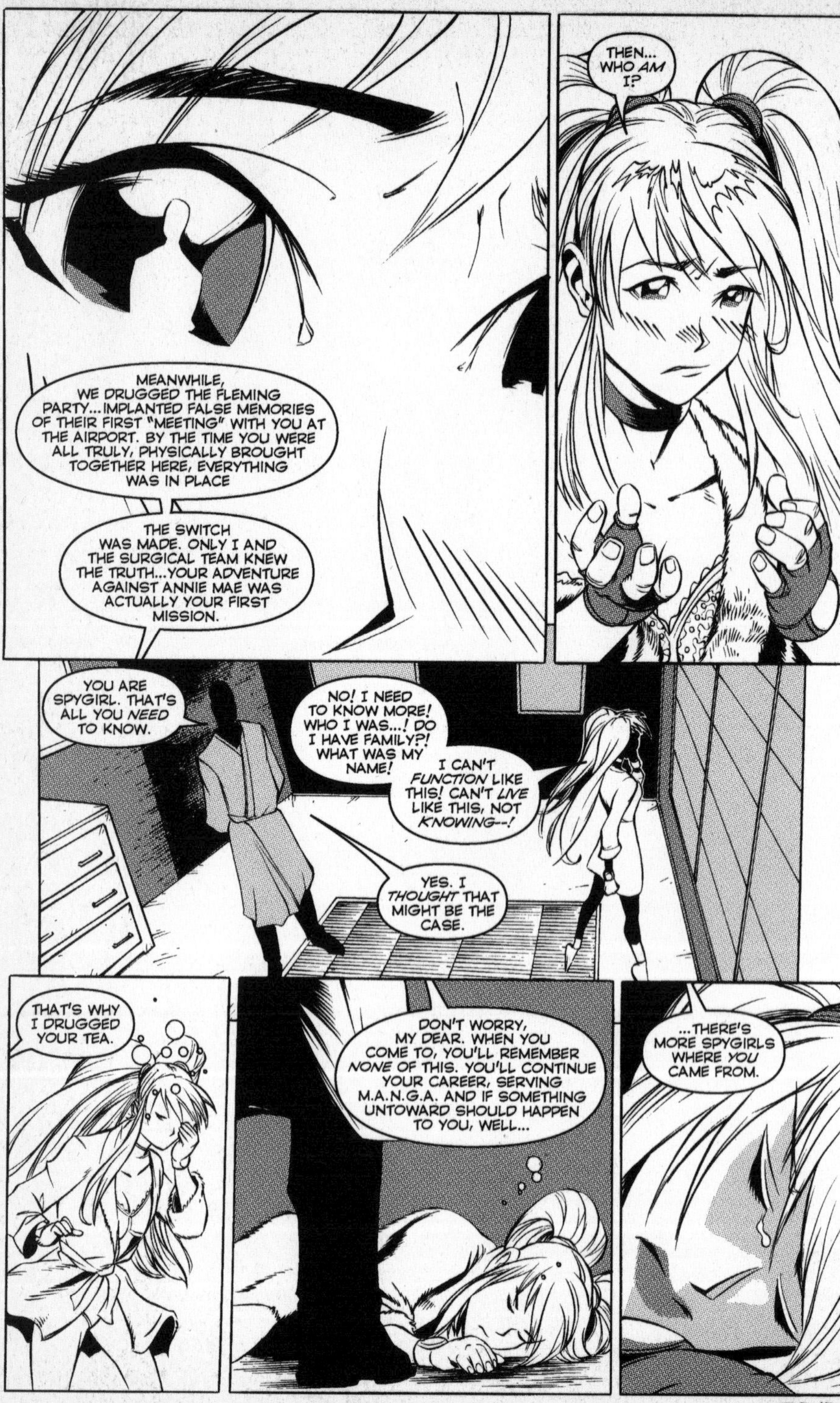
MEANWHILE, WE DRUGGED THE FLEMING PARTY...IMPLANTED FALSE MEMORIES OF THEIR FIRST "MEETING" WITH YOU AT THE AIRPORT. BY THE TIME YOU WERE ALL TRULY, PHYSICALLY BROUGHT TOGETHER HERE, EVERYTHING WAS IN PLACE
THE SWITCH WAS MADE. ONLY I AND THE SURGICAL TEAM KNEW THE TRUTH...YOUR ADVENTURE AGAINST ANNIE MAE WAS ACTUALLY YOUR FIRST MISSION.
THEN... WHO *AM* I?
YOU ARE SPYGIRL. THAT'S ALL YOU *NEED* TO KNOW.
NO! I NEED TO KNOW MORE! WHO I WAS...! DO I HAVE FAMILY?! WHAT WAS MY NAME!
I CAN'T *FUNCTION* LIKE THIS! CAN'T *LIVE* LIKE THIS, NOT *KNOWING*--!
YES. I *THOUGHT* THAT MIGHT BE THE CASE.
THAT'S WHY I DRUGGED YOUR TEA.
DON'T WORRY, MY DEAR. WHEN YOU COME TO, YOU'LL REMEMBER *NONE* OF THIS. YOU'LL CONTINUE YOUR CAREER, SERVING M.A.N.G.A. AND IF SOMETHING UNTOWARD SHOULD HAPPEN TO YOU, WELL...
...THERE'S MORE SPYGIRLS WHERE *YOU* CAME FROM.

END

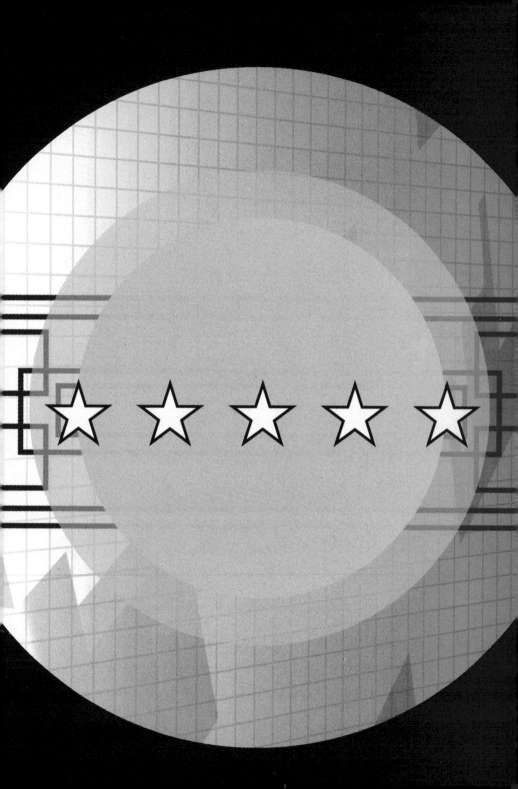

DARK HORSE GIVES YOU THE BEST MANGA THIS SIDE OF THE RISING SUN!

AKIRA
Katsuhiro Otomo

Book 1
1-56971-498-3 $24.95

Book 2
1-56971-499-1 $24.95

Book 3
1-56971-525-4 $24.95

Book 4
1-56971-526-2 $27.95

Book 5
1-56971-527-0 $27.95

Book 6
1-56971-528-9 $29.95

ASTRO BOY
Osamu Tezuka

Volume 1
1-56971-676-5 $9.95

Volume 2
1-56971-677-3 $9.95

Volume 3
1-56971-678-1 $9.95

Volume 4
1-56971-679-X $9.95

Volume 5
1-56971-680-3 $9.95

Volume 6
1-56971-681-1 $9.95

Volume 7
1-56971-790-7 $9.95

Volume 8
1-56971-791-5 $9.95

Volume 9
1-56971-792-3 $9.95

Volume 10
1-56971-793-1 $9.95

Volume 11
1-56971-812-1 $9.95

Volume 12
1-56971-813-X $9.95

Volume 13
1-56971-894-6 $9.95

Volume 14
1-56971-895-4 $9.95

Volume 15
1-56971-896-2 $9.95

Volume 16
1-56971-897-0 $9.95

Volume 17
1-56971-898-9 $9.95

Volume 18
1-56971-899-7 $9.95

Volume 19
1-56971-900-4 $9.95

Volume 20
1-56971-901-2 $9.95

BLADE OF THE IMMORTAL
Hiroaki Samura

Blood of a Thousand
1-56971-239-5 $14.95

Cry of The Worm
1-56971-300-6 $14.95

Dreamsong
1-56971-357-X $14.95

On Silent Wings
1-56971-412-6 $14.95

On Silent Wings II
1-56971-444-4 $14.95

Dark Shadows
1-56971-469-X $14.95

Heart of Darkness
1-56971-531-9 $16.95

The Gathering
1-56971-546-7 $15.95

The Gathering II
1-56971-560-2 $15.95

Beasts
1-56971-741-9 $14.95

Secrets
1-56971-746-X $16.95

CANNON GOD EXAXXION
Kenichi Sonoda

STAGE 1
1-56971-745-1 $15.95

STAGE 2
1-56971-966-7 $14.95

CLUB 9
Makoto Kobayashi

Book 1
1-56971-915-2 $15.95

Book 2
1-56971-968-3 $15.95

DOMU: A CHILD'S DREAM
Katsuhiro Otomo
1-56971-611-0 $17.95

GHOST IN THE SHELL
Masamune Shirow
1-56971-081-3 $24.95

GUNSMITH CATS
Kenichi Sonoda

Bonnie and Clyde
1-56971-215-8 $13.95

Misfire
1-56971-253-0 $14.95

The Return of Gray
1-56971-299-9 $17.95

Goldie vs. Misty
1-56971-371-5 $15.95

Bad Trip
1-56971-442-8 $13.95

Bean Bandit
1-56971-453-3 $16.95

Kidnapped
1-56971-529-7 $16.95

Mr. V
1-56971-550-5 $18.95

Misty's Run
1-56971-684-6 $14.95

INTRON DEPOT
Masamune Shirow

Intron Depot 1
1-56971-085-6 $39.95

Intron Depot 2: Blades
1-56971-382-0 $39.95

LONE WOLF AND CUB
Kazuo Koike & Goseki Kojima
Collect the complete 28-volume series!

Volume 1: The Assassin's Road
1-56971-502-5 $9.95

Volume 2: The Gateless Barrier
1-56971-503-3 $9.95

Volume 3: The Flute Of The Fallen Tiger
1-56971-504-1 $9.95

Volume 4: The Bell Warden
1-56971-505-X $9.95

Volume 5: Black Wind
1-5671-506-8 $9.95

Volume 6: Lanterns for the Dead
1-56971-507-6 $9.95

Volume 7: Cloud Dragon, Wind Tiger
1-56971-508-4 $9.95

Volume 8: Chains Of Death
1-56971-509-2 $9.95

Volume 9: Echo Of The Assassin
1-56971-510-6 $9.95

Volume 10: Hostage Child
1-56971-511-4 $9.95

Volume 11: Talisman Of Hades
1-56971-512-2 $9.95

Volume 12: Shattered Stones
1-56971-513-0 $9.95

Volume 13: The Moon In The East, The Sun In The West
1-56971-585-8 $9.95

Volume 14: Day Of The Demons
1-56971-586-6 $9.95

Volume 15: Brothers Of The Grass
1-56971-587-4 $9.95

Volume 16: Gateway Into Winter
1-56971-588-2 $9.95

Volume 17: The Will Of The Fang
1-56971-589-0 $9.95

Volume 18: Twilight Of The Kurokuwa
1-56971-590-4 $9.95

Volume 19: The Moon In Our Hearts
1-56971-591-2 $9.95

Volume 20: A Taste Of Poison
1-56971-592-0 $9.95

Volume 21: Fragrance Of Death
1-56971-593-9 $9.95

Volume 22: Heaven And Earth
1-56971-594-7 $9.95

Volume 23: Tears Of Ice
1-56971-595-5 $9.95

Volume 24: In These Small Hands
1-56971-596-3 $9.95

Volume 25: Perhaps In Death
1-56971-597-1 $9.95

Volume 26: Struggle In The Dark
1-56971-598-X $9.95

Volume 27: Battle's Eve
1-56971-599-8 $9.95

Volume 28: The Lotus Throne
1-56971-600-5 $9.95

OH MY GODDESS!
Kosuke Fujishima

Wrong Number
1-56971-669-2 $13.95

Love Potion No. 9
1-56971-252-2 $14.95

Sympathy For The Devil
1-56971-329-4 $13.95

Terrible Master Urd
1-56971-369-3 $14.95

Adventures Of The Mini-Goddesses
1-56971-421-5 $9.95

The Queen Of Vengeance
1-56971-431-2 $13.95

Mara Strikes Back!
1-56971-449-5 $14.95

Ninja Master
1-56971-474-6 $13.95

Miss Keiichi
1-56971-522-X $16.95

The Devil In Miss Urd
1-56971-540-8 $14.95

The Fourth Goddess
1-56971-551-3 $18.95

Childhood's End
1-56971-685-4 $15.95

Queen Sayoko
1-56971-766-4 $16.95

Hand In Hand
1-56971-921-7 $17.95

Mystery Child
1-56971-950-0 $17.95

OUTLANDERS
Johji Manabe

Volume 1
1-56971-161-5 $13.95

Volume 2
1-56971-162-3 $13.95

Volume 3
1-56971-163-1 $13.95

Volume 4
1-56971-069-4 $12.95

Volume 5
1-56971-275-1 $14.95

Volume 6
1-56971-423-1 $14.95

Volume 7
1-56971-424-X $14.95

Volume 8
1-56971-425-8 $14.95

SERAPHIC FEATHER
Hiroyuki Utatane • Yo Morimoto

Volume 1: Crimson Angel
1-56971-555-6 $17.95

Volume 2: Seeds Of Chaos
1-56971-739-7 $17.95

Volume 3: Target Zone
1-56971-912-8 $17.95

Volume 4: Dark Angel
1-56971-913-6 $17.95

SHADOW LADY
Masakazu Katsura

Dangerous Love
1-56971-408-8 $17.95

The Awakening
1-56971-446-0 $15.95

Sudden Death
1-56971-477-0 $14.95

SHADOW STAR
Mohiro Kitoh

Volume 1: Starflight
1-56971-548-3 $15.95

Volume 2: Darkness Visible
1-56971-740-0 $14.95

Volume 3:
Shadows Of The Past
1-56971-743-5 $13.95

Volume 4:
Nothing But The Truth
1-56971-920-9 $14.95

3X3 EYES
Yuzo Takada

House Of Demons
1-56971- 931-4 $14.95

Curse Of The Gesu
1-56971-930-6 $14.95

Flight Of The Demon
1-56971-553-X $15.95

Blood Of The Sacred Demon
1-56971-735-4 $13.95

Summoning Of The Beast
1-56971-747-8 $14.95

WHAT'S MICHAEL?
Makoto Kobayashi

Book 5:
What's Michael's Favorite Spot?
1-56971-557-2 $8.95

Book 6:
Hard Day's Life
1-56971-744-3 $8.95

Book 7:
Fat Cat In The City
1-56971-914-4 $8.95

DARK HORSE MANGA

AVAILABLE AT YOUR LOCAL COMICS SHOP OR BOOKSTORE!

To find a comics shop in your area, call 1-888-266-4226
For more information or to order direct:
• On the web: www.darkhorse.com • Email: mailorder@darkhorse.com
• Phone: 1-800-962-0052 Mon.-Sat. 9 A.M. to 5 P.M. Pacific Time
*Prices and availability subject to change without notice

Mike Richardson publisher • Neil Hankerson executive vice president • Tom Weddle vice president of finance • Randy Stradley vice president of publishing • Chris Warner senior books editor • Sara Perrin vice president of marketing • Michael Martens vice president of business development • Anita Nelson vice president of sales & licensing • David Scroggy vice president of product development • Mark Cox art director • Dale LaFountain vice president of information technology • Darlene Vogel director of purchasing • Ken Lizzi general counsel

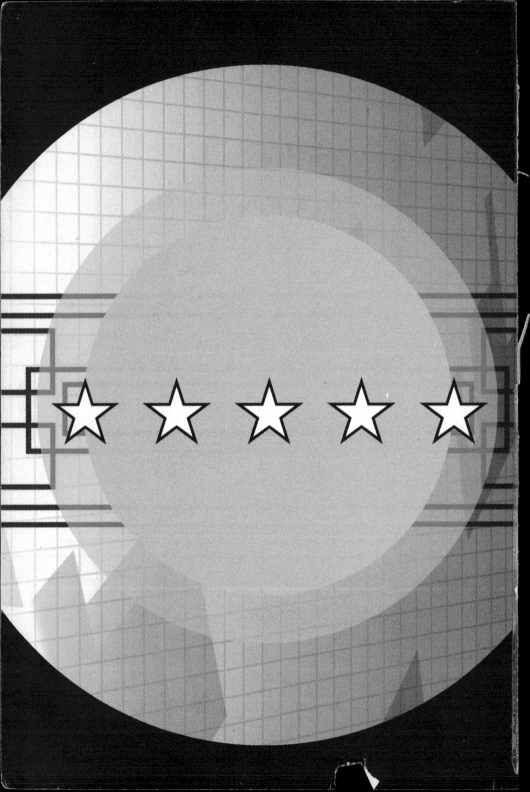